Praise for

The Nurse's Gra...

D0891347

"Grantwriting can be a daunting task for the novice and experienced nurse alike. In *The Nurse's Grantwriting Advantage*, Dr. Bowers-Lanier takes the nurse through the entire process of grantwriting—from problem identification, to concept paper, to searching for grantwriting opportunities, to actually submitting the application—in a way that demystifies the process. Full of tips, checklists, and take-away points, this text is the only guidebook any nurse needs to navigate the grantwriting process."

–Cynthia Armstrong Persily, PhD, RN, FAAN
Professor and Associate Dean
West Virginia University School of Nursing

"*The Nurse's Grantwriting Advantage* is a must-read for those seeking grant funding. I love how it starts with the end in mind—first looking at the proposal from the funder or reviewer point of view. The text clearly outlines the steps in writing a proposal, along with providing quick links for finding further detail."

–Susan Boyer, MEd, RN, FAHCEP
Executive Director, VT Nurses In Partnership

"*The Nurse's Grantwriting Advantage* is a must-have for novice to beginner grantwriters who are seeking funding success. Becky Bowers-Lanier has created a captivating book that is easy to read, humorous, and practical. All necessary topics are covered with helpful take-away messages scattered throughout the book. The layout of each chapter follows a logical design from key terms, useful tips, and FAQs."

–Anne M. McNamara, PhD, RN
Dean and Professor of Nursing
College of Nursing and Health Sciences
Grand Canyon University

"Dr. Bowers-Lanier clearly demonstrates her skill as a teacher, leader, collaborator, and joyful companion through adventures in successful fundraising for nursing! And I love her quotes! I am looking forward to sharing this very motivating and instructive book with colleagues committed to attracting funding to support innovations and research in nursing."

–Ellen Canepa Brzytwa, MSN, MPH, RN
Health Consultant
Cleveland, Ohio

"*The Nurse's Grantwriting Advantage* provides a clear process, suggestions, and basic tips to help any nurse develop successful grant requests. Nurses interested in funding ideas to improve patient care or their workplace should read this book!"

–Dennis R. Sherrod, EdD, RN
Director of Graduate Programs
Professor and Forsyth Medical Center
Endowed Chair of Recruitment & Retention
Winston-Salem State University, Division of Nursing

The Nurse's Grant Writing Advantage

How Grantwriting Can Advance Your Nursing Career

By Rebecca Bowers-Lanier, EdD, MSN, MPH, RN

Sigma Theta Tau International
Honor Society of Nursing

Sigma Theta Tau International

The Honor Society of Nursing, Sigma Theta Tau International (STTI) is a nonprofit organization whose mission is to support the learning, knowledge, and professional development of nurses committed to making a difference in health worldwide. Founded in 1922, STTI has 130,000 members in 86 countries. Members include practicing nurses, instructors, researchers, policymakers, entrepreneurs and others. STTI's 470 chapters are located at 586 institutions of higher education throughout Australia, Botswana, Brazil, Canada, Colombia, Ghana, Hong Kong, Japan, Kenya, Malawi, Mexico, the Netherlands, Pakistan, Singapore, South Africa, South Korea, Swaziland, Sweden, Taiwan, Tanzania, the United States, and Wales. More information about STTI can be found online at www.nursingsociety.org.

Sigma Theta Tau International
550 West North Street
Indianapolis, IN 46202

To order additional books, buy in bulk, or order for corporate use, contact Nursing Knowledge International at 888.NKI.4YOU (888.654.4968/US and Canada) or +1.317.634.8171 (outside US and Canada).

To request a review copy for course adoption, e-mail solutions@nursingknowledge.org or call 888.NKI.4YOU (888.654.4968/US and Canada) or +1.317.917.4983 (outside US and Canada).

To request author information, or for speaker or other media requests, contact Rachael McLaughlin of the Honor Society of Nursing, Sigma Theta Tau International at 888.634.7575 (US and Canada) or +1.317.634.8171 (outside US and Canada).

ISBNs
Print: 978-1-935476-73-3
EPUB/Mobi: 978-1-935476-74-0
PDF: 978-1-935476-75-7

Library of Congress Cataloging-in-Publication Data

Bowers-Lanier, Rebecca, 1944–
The nurse's grantwriting advantage / Rebecca Bowers-Lanier.
     p. ; cm.
Includes bibliographical references.
ISBN 978-1-935476-73-3 (alk. paper)
I. Sigma Theta Tau International. II. Title.
[DNLM: 1. Financing, Organized--United States. 2. Nursing Research--United States. 3. Fellowships and Scholarships--United States. 4. Research Design--United States. 5. Research Support as Topic--United States. 6. Writing--United States. WY 20.5]
LC classification not assigned
                              808.06661--dc23
2011040127

First Printing, 2012

Publisher: Renee Wilmeth
Project Editor: Brian Herrmann
Copy Editor: Deb Buehler
Indexer: Jane Palmer
Original Cover Design: Studio Galou
Cover Design: Katy Bodenmiller

Principal Book Editor: Carla Hall
Editorial Coordinator: Paula Jeffers
Proofreader: Barbara Bennett
Interior Design and Page Layout:
Rebecca Batchelor

Dedication

To my parents, Gert and Jake Bowers, who at 90 years of age, continue to be role models for integrity, intellectual curiosity, humor, and a deep appreciation for the human condition.

Acknowledgements

Thanks to Carla Hall, Brian Herrmann, Renee Wilmeth, and everyone at Sigma Theta Tau International for providing me with this opportunity to put in words what I have learned about proposal writing throughout my career. Thanks also to the individuals who suggested ideas for the clinical and educational examples I used in the book. These include Phyllis Whitehead, PhD, RN, CNS, and Rebecca Culver Clark, PhD, RN, of the Carilion Clinic in Roanoke, Virginia, and Paula Saxby, PhD, RN, of the Virginia Board of Nursing. James McIntosh of Nonsense at Work (nonsenseatwork.com) served as a sounding board and positive influence in nudging me forward. Finally, my husband, Jack, deserves many thanks for his forbearance on the weekends as I buried myself in the manuscript.

About the Author

Rebecca Bowers-Lanier

Rebecca Bowers-Lanier, EdD, MPH, MSN, RN, is president of B2L Consulting in Richmond, Virginia, where she works as an advocacy consultant at the state level for nonprofits in health care and public education. From 1995 until 2003, she served as deputy director of Colleagues in Caring: Regional Collaboratives for Nursing Workforce Development, a national program funded by The Robert Wood Johnson Foundation. She has more than 20 years of experience as a nurse educator and nursing program administrator, having taught at the diploma, associate, baccalaureate, and master's levels. She has worked on successful grantwriting and administration of national, statewide, and local grants.

Bowers-Lanier holds bachelor's and master's degrees in nursing from the University of Pennsylvania, where she was a member and president of Xi Chapter, Sigma Theta Tau International. She has a master's in public health from Virginia Commonwealth University, and a doctorate in higher education administration from the College of William and Mary in Virginia. She is a past president of the Virginia Nurses Association and a former board member of the Center for American Nursing.

Table of Contents

Foreword

"To give away money is an easy matter and in any man's power. But to decide to whom to give it and how large and when, and for what purpose and how, is neither in every man's power nor an easy matter."

"Know how to ask. There is nothing more difficult for some people nor for others, easier."

–Baltasar Gracian

As a foundation program officer, I've often heard people say, "What a great job, giving away money—how fun!" The truth is that being on the giving side of the nonprofit world is a great job. It can also be fun. There are few things more exhilarating than calling an applicant and announcing that the project has been funded. People respond with great joy and sometimes tears; occasionally someone is speechless. Being thanked profusely does wonders for my day, even if it is not my own money, and even if it is a small amount. Even a small amount of money in the right place at the right time can move mountains. Helping others to do good work to improve the social condition is rewarding for everyone involved, whether it's by awarding financial support or participating as a community partner in the change effort.

On the flip side, saying no to a project is often the hardest thing a program officer has to face. We couch it as "declining the proposal" rather than "rejecting the project," although we know that it feels the same to the applicant. Sometimes the proposal submitted was unclear, confusing, vague, or simply poorly written, making us work extra hard to understand the meaning and potential value. We try to overlook these things and understand how difficult it is for people who are inspired by an idea to put into words what they need and what they want to do. Other proposals are beautifully crafted, but the project itself seems poorly designed or is missing key elements for success. We often have very little time to dig deeper and figure out the missing meaning, so we remove the proposal from consideration to make way for those that we find easier to understand.

People usually ask for special tips to ensure funding. Consistently, I have only a few to share. The first is not to underestimate the power of a narrative story. Stories have been shared in every culture as a means of entertainment, education, cultural preservation, and persuasion throughout history. Within philanthropy, using fiction storytelling techniques to communicate can be more compelling and effective than using only dry facts. Instead of telling me that 37,000 people will be better off because of your project, tell me about one person whose life is forever changed by the activities you have outlined in the proposal. Using a fictionalized (or true) story interprets the past and current circumstances for me and shapes the future (how I perceive your work). For your grant application to be successful, I have to see myself in your story. Once I understand the narrative, I can be convinced of the rightness of the funding. The more complex the situation, the easier it is for me to be involved in the outcomes and the harder it is for me to say no to your proposal.

In the chapters that follow, Rebecca Bowers-Lanier describes a comprehensive and sophisticated method for clearly articulating your project goals and objectives to lead to a successful grant. She begins with my second tip: Understand the grant GIVING process—this is an important perspective for potential grantwriters, and you should spend some time reviewing Chapter 1 in detail. Like you, foundation reviewers face competing demands for their money, time, and attention. Developing a grant application by imagining being on the other side is a creative way to understand the process and the importance of adhering to the steps required for good proposal writing. What would you want to know in order to give money to an idea? How would you be persuaded? Even if you are not part of a giving circle, you can use these insights to support your own personal charitable giving activities. Understanding how foundations work is critical to your grantwriting.

Likewise, the author describes the importance of developing a concept paper. My third tip is to create the concept paper well before you begin to look for funding sources, as it will help you to think through the problem and to review the possible solutions. Applicants often focus too soon on one approach when there may be many ways to solve a challenge. Your concept paper is your guiding document, and you want it to stand on its own and be something you can refer to as you develop proposals to multiple foundations and for use with potential partners or media strategies. Additionally, it is helpful to get feedback from a friend or colleague before submitting a concept paper to a potential funder. If someone who is not familiar with your project can understand what you've written, then it's likely you've done a good enough job for a foundation program officer to understand. The importance of concept papers cannot be overstated.

My final tip to you as a new grantwriter is to go beyond the goals and objectives, beyond logic models and technical skills, and write with your heart. As a grantmaker, I can tell you that I know when someone has written with passion and commitment to the project. I know when your pet peeve has become your cause by the way you inspire me to join in your efforts. I like the experience of reading a proposal and being intrigued by the story enough to want to know more. I have often met applicants and was so impressed by the passion and commitment of the individuals that I knew that somehow, someway, the project would be successful with or without our foundation funds. A grantmaking mentor of mine once said that we often make funding choices when we feel magic in the proposal. Bowers-Lanier has created an excellent primer to teach you the skills to write an excellent grant. Take your heartfelt desires for something better than what you see, take the lessons from this book to help articulate your vision, and help others to feel your magic.

–Judith Woodruff, JD
Program Director
Northwest Health Foundation

Introduction

Years ago, when I was a young nursing faculty member, I marveled at my colleagues' abilities to write proposals for grants. To me, the uninitiated, it seemed like they possessed magical skills—somehow they could envision an idea and find someone to pay for it. I wanted to learn how to write proposals and obtain grant funding.

Consequently, I went to a grantwriting workshop. Then I went to another grantwriting workshop. Then I purchased a book on grantwriting. Nothing happened. No grantwriting opportunity fell into my lap, perhaps because I was unclear about where to start.

Several years ensued, and I found myself in a faculty position at Hampton University in Hampton, Virginia. Our dean, Dr. Elnora Daniel, was mythical in her ability to obtain grant funding. I was ready and eager to learn from the master. Elnora put me to work, and I quickly found that there was no myth to writing proposals—merely working on ideas, determining the logic of project planning, and putting ideas and logic into words.

At Hampton, we adhered to a formula for proposal writing that most often led to success. We worked in teams, parsing out the components of the proposals and assigning individuals portions to write. The team developed the overall project goal and objectives; each person determined the action steps and narrative to complement the work plan. One person assumed responsibility for putting the entire proposal together in time for mailing to the grantmaker.

Over the years, I've become adept at writing proposals, and I find the process to be exhilarating and enormously creative. I've also been fortunate to manage a project funded by The Robert Wood Johnson Foundation, and in that role, I have written calls for proposals, provided technical assistance to individuals and groups working on their response to the calls, and monitored funded projects for compliance. So I have participated in almost every aspect of the grant business, except for actually raising the funds for making grants.

This book is written for you, the novice grantwriter. I have tried to shed light on any myths you might have about grantwriting. The book is designed to provide you with an overall picture of how proposals are written from beginning to end. However, you don't necessarily have to read it from beginning to end in that order. I do recommend that you start with Chapter 1, because I put you in the grantor's place so you can see early on how the process works—in reverse. If you can visualize yourself as a grantor, you can become a proposal writer.

Obtaining grant funding is one means of supporting projects that otherwise might not be funded. Today's parsimonious fiscal climate leaves very little excess to fund creative approaches to pedagogy for solving perplexing clinical problems. Finding charitable organizations whose missions support the ideas you want to test is a worthy endeavor—not only for you but ultimately for the impact your project might have on students and/or clients.

Read on, and best wishes on your journey toward becoming an excellent, successful proposal writer!

Quiz

1. You are a staff nurse on a medical-surgical floor. The staff on your unit has determined that all patients with intravenous lines will receive a certain type of care to the IV site to prevent infection. In your previous staff position, the agency used another IV site care method that you believe is superior to the one currently used in your new facility. Which of the following approaches should you use to determine which method is preferable?

A. Show your manager the procedure manual from your previous employer to convince this person of your assessment.

B. Complain loudly about the current method with your fellow staff nurses.

C. Engage your peers in learning about both methods, and discuss ways to find out which method is preferable.

D. Drop your complaints and acquiesce to the procedure in your current unit.

Correct answer: C. Involve others in learning about other approaches. These individuals may become allies in helping you solve a problem.

2. How can writing a grant proposal help you determine which IV site care method has better outcomes? If you are awarded funds, you will be able to (circle all that apply):

A. Establish a research project designed to find which method has better outcomes.

B. Obtain the resources to purchase supplies needed to find the answer.

C. Include your peers in the research process.

D. Write up your results and present the findings to administrators, professional associations, and other interested parties.

Correct answer: All of the above. Obtaining funds to support research not only helps you find answers to clinical problems, but also engages others in the research process and promotes both your participation and theirs in presenting the results.

3. True or false: Working with others in solving clinical or educational problems is an important component of the process of developing a concept paper and submitting a proposal.

Correct answer: True. Writing concept papers and proposals is a team sport best done with a group of individuals who can contribute in individual ways. The process is messier and more complex, but the product is richer for it.

4. For which of the following reasons should you conduct a needs assessment for a clinical or educational problem?

A. To determine the extent of a problem.

B. To find out if others need your involvement.

C. To assess the ability of your peers to solve a problem.

D. To learn about the importance of collecting data.

Correct answer: A. Needs assessments help determine the extent of a problem. If you plan to search for funds to support your problem solving, you will need to demonstrate to the funder that there is a need to solve the problem.

5. All of the following, except one, are important rules to follow when seeking funds to support the resolution of a clinical or educational problem. Which is NOT a rule you should follow?

A. Working with potential funders involves exquisite interpersonal communications.

B. Get to know grantmakers before you need them.

C. Find the money first; then find your problem.

D. Match your problem with the grantmaker's mission and funding priorities.

Correct answer: C. Start with a problem, then look for possible solutions and funding sources, not the other way around.

6. Complete the following matching exercise, linking synonyms of terms used in grantwriting to describe how a project will be designed and implemented.

1	Activities	A	Impact
2	Goal	B	Objectives
3	Outputs	C	Action steps
4	Inputs	D	Deliverables
5	Outcomes	E	Resources

Answers: 1/Activities and C/Action steps; 2/Goal and A/Impact; 3/Outputs and D/Deliverables; 4/Inputs and E/Resources; 5/Outcomes and B/Objectives.

7. Which of the following types of evaluation do you conduct at the completion of a project? (Select two.)

A. Process evaluation

B. Context evaluation

C. Input evaluation

D. Product evaluation

E. Summative evaluation

Correct answers: D and E are the terms that answer the question about whether the proposed activities designed to solve a problem actually achieved their goal.

8. True or false: A proposal budget should mirror the proposal narrative.

Correct answer: True. The line-item budget and the budget narrative should be internally consistent with the proposal's impact, resources, inputs, outputs, and outcomes.

Quiz   xix

9. True or false: Proposal writing is a synonym for creative writing.

Correct answer: False. Proposal writing should be conducted according to the grantmaker's specific instructions in regard to page length, line spacing, and font size.

10. Which of the following purposes do site visits serve? Check all that apply.

A. Clarify if there are gaps or confusing portions of the proposal.

B. Amplify or provide opportunities for the applicant to further explain what is written.

C. Verify the accuracy of the contents of the proposal.

Correct answer: All of them are reasons for site visits.

1

✳

Grantmaking in Reverse:
Awarding Grants Through Giving Circles

Do you:

Know about giving circles?

Know to whom grant money is given?

Know how to write a proposal application?

Know how to award money to the best applicant?

Grantwriting can be a daunting task for those who have never taken the journey. In this chapter, we examine the process in reverse, asking you, the reader, to be the grantmaker. Looking at it from this perspective will help demystify the process by putting you in the grantmaker's place. We do this from the perspective of giving circles.

Glossary

Applicant: An organization seeking grant funds for a specific project.

Giving circle: A form of philanthropy consisting of groups of individuals who pool their funds and resources to donate to their communities (www.michiganfoundations.org/s_cmf/sec.asp).

Grant: A sum of money given to an organization for a specific purpose.

Grantee: The recipient of a grant.

Grantmaker: An organization that makes a grant. Also called grantor.

Call or request for proposals (commonly abbreviated as CFP or RFP): A document that describes a project and seeks applicants to submit a written response detailing their plan to carry out the specifics of the project.

Needs assessment: A process for gathering information about current conditions within a population that underlie the need for an intervention (www.epa.gov/evaluate/glossary/all-esd.htm). Usually forms the basis for an intervention plan.

Philanthropy: The desire to promote the welfare of others, usually expressed by a donation of money to good causes.

Proposal: A term used to describe an intention or a plan to accomplish something.

Technical assistance: Help and advice provided on a specialized subject matter (www.nonprofitsassistancefund.org/index.php).

Becoming a philanthropist

"It is more blessed to give than to receive."

—Acts 20:35

Suppose you and several of your friends form a club designed to give money to your favorite causes, a so-called giving circle. For the purposes of this example, we'll call our giving circle Action for Healthy Community, or AHC.

What's the brief history of giving circles?

Giving circles emerged in the 1990s and have gained in numbers and interest since. As of 2007, the Forum of Regional Associations of Grantmakers counted more than 400 giving circles across the nation (Bearman, 2007). Simply put, a giving circle is a group of individuals who pool their dollars, decide where to give the money (and other resources, such as volunteer time), and learn together about their community and philanthropy (Bearman, 2007). Although data are not available about nurses' involvement in giving circles, more than likely nurses are circle members because of their commitment to serving others.

Why do people establish giving circles?

As the description implies, people form giving circles to raise and donate money to causes. Raising money takes many forms, including individual donations and other forms of fundraising. Because of their investment of time, money, and energy, circle members uniformly want to spend their money wisely, and hence, they develop stipulations on how they will invest their money.

TIP

It's your money; spend it wisely.

Giving away your money

"We can find meaning and reward by serving some higher purpose than ourselves, a shining purpose, the illumination of a Thousand Points of Light... We all have something to give."

—George H.W. Bush, 41st President of the United States

How do giving circles decide where to give their money?

You have joined AHC, whose purpose is to promote healthy communities, because it is congruent with your own beliefs about worthy causes. In your community, like most communities, opportunities abound for improving its health, from increasing accessibility for persons with disabilities to improving maternal-infant mortality through nutritional programs and so forth. With so many community health issues, your circle possesses the daunting task of narrowing its philanthropic purpose.

TIP

Be clear about how you want the money to be used to achieve its intended outcome.

In our hypothetical situation, your circle decides to put its money and energy into children's health and specifically healthy nutritional habits. Therefore, you decide that the target of your grant giving will be tax-exempt entities that focus on children's health, childhood nutrition, or related interests. Your circle has accepted member donations for 2 years and has $2,000 to invest.

What items form the basis of a call for proposals?

As AHC members crystallize their thoughts about how to spend the circle's money, they develop a brief mission/vision statement for the project itself, such as the example below. This statement forms the basis for how AHC will review proposals and award its grant.

Goal: Improve child nutrition in community.

Objective: Educate children and families about healthy food selections.

Target: Preschool through grade 5 children and their families.

Measure: At least one educational program will be established with acceptable numbers of involved children and families, consistent with funds available.

These four items—goal, objective, target, and measure—form the basis for the giving circle to develop its application materials. Understanding that $2,000 is not a lot of money and that the grant recipient is likely to be a small, nonprofit entity, AHC will develop a short, concise application that requires the applicants to demonstrate how they will achieve the grant objective with the funds awarded. AHC's task is to make the application clear and to the point.

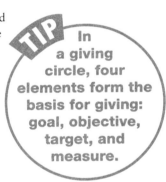

TIP In a giving circle, four elements form the basis for giving: goal, objective, target, and measure.

What additional information will help a giving circle determine the best applicant?

Here are the items that AHC will ask to be included in its call for proposals:

* A statement of the problem with goals and objectives for carrying out the work.

* A description of the applying organization including history, successful management of other grants, and demographics of people receiving services; leadership and organizational structure identifying expertise in the subject matter; resources the

applicant plans to invest in the project; and methods by which the applicant will measure and publicly report the successful completion of the project being proposed.

* A needs assessment in support of the necessity of the project from the applicant's perspective.

* A description of the target population who will benefit from the project.

* An action plan to accomplish the project objective; what the applicant proposes to do, who will be involved, the timeline for completion, and how the applicant will measure attainment of the objective.

* A budget description, including how the applicant will allocate granted funds to accomplish project objectives.

AHC may also set certain requirements for the proposals, including the following:

* Length, margins, fonts, and spacing

* Deadline for submission

* Type of submission (electronic or paper copy)

TIP Be sure to include everything in your call for proposals that will help you find the best applicant to receive your funds.

Finally, AHC members should develop an assessment methodology that will help them decide on worthy applications. This might include a check-off list, a series of questions to be answered, or a table with the requirements and a weight assigned to each part of the proposal. Box 1.1 contains a sample of how an assessment methodology might look, if in the form of questions to be answered.

(1.1) Proposal evaluation criteria

* Does the applicant adequately describe its ability to carry out the project?

* Are the proposal's goals and objectives congruent with the AHC mission?

* Do the goals and objectives have measurable outcomes and a plan to measure the outcomes?

* Is the project population clearly identified?

* Does the applicant describe the need for the project?

* Does the applicant describe how it will achieve the outcomes?

* Is the budget consistent with the project's strategies?

* Does the applicant adhere to the AHC requirements for length, font, margins, and spacing?

* Was the application delivered on time?

How will you determine the best recipient of your money?

Once AHC has developed its application, it will disseminate it among potential applicants in the community. The next step will be to review the applications received and schedule meetings with the finalists.

Once the proposals have been publicized, applicants may seek clarification from AHC members. Members should decide in advance how much technical assistance they will offer to applicants. Technical assistance may take the form of formal meetings with all applicants, answering questions via electronic means or in person, and/or reviewing drafts of proposals and providing feedback. Remember, the idea is to make the best use of AHC money, so the more the applicant can assure AHC that it will be a good steward of the grant money, the more likely the project will be successful.

TIP Be prudent in selecting the applicant whose proposal demonstrates the greatest ability to achieve the intended outcome of the grant award.

Once applications are received, AHC members will perform two types of proposal review: (1) a cursory review to make sure that application requirements are met, including margins, fonts, and so forth, as well as component parts of the proposal; and (2) a more in-depth review to determine whether the submitted plans are likely to achieve the stated project outcome. The in-depth review is probably the most nerve-wracking phase for both the grantors and the applicants. The AHC circle members want to award the grant to the most worthy applicant; the applicants want to receive the award by submitting the very best application.

AHC members may want to meet with the top finalists through site visits. In site visits, circle members visit with the applicants in their settings, such as schools or clinics. The visit provides the grantors with an opportunity to observe the following:

* The applicants' familiarity with the proposed project

* The applicants' interactions with one another

* The physical environment of the setting itself

* The capacity of staff to run the daily operations of the organization, as well as their potential to implement the proposed project

What happens after the grant is awarded?

After site visits and proposal reviews of the finalists, AHC members will decide on the final award recipient. The award recipient becomes the grantee, and circle members will make final arrangements for handling of the grant money, reporting of activity on the project, and other logistics involved with successful completion of the project.

After all is said and done, the most rewarding part of grantmaking begins, for both the grantors and the grantees. The grantmakers (AHC) will monitor the progress of how the grantees are spending the granted funds to achieve the goals of the project, and the grantees will work diligently to be good stewards of AHC's grant. The real winners are the target population and whether their nutritional status is improved through the work of the project.

References

Bearman, J. E. (2007). *More giving together: The growth and impact of giving circles and shared giving.* Forum of Regional Associations of Grantmakers. Retrieved from http://www.givingforum.org/s_forum/index.asp

TAKE-AWAY TIPS

✓ **If you are in the grantmaker role, you want to make sure that your money will be well spent, so you should be clear about your giving goals and who will benefit from the contribution.**

✓ **Write a call for proposals that articulates the intention of the project and the specifics of what must be included in the proposals, as well as who is eligible to apply.**

✓ **Offer technical assistance to applicants seeking help with their proposals. You'll be more likely to get what you are seeking, and they will be better prepared to submit a proposal that matches your funding priority.**

✓ **Be fair in grading proposals. To be completely fair, share with the applicants the tool you will use in evaluating their proposals. Keep the process transparent.**

✓ **Feel good about yourself for participating as a philanthropist. In a small way you are working to make your community healthier.**

FAQs

 Is grantmaking more fun than grantwriting?

"Fun" is in the eye of the beholder. Giving circles bring together individuals who want to contribute to the common good, however that is defined in their community. These individuals are passionate about making their communities better, donating time and money toward efforts by others to improve the community. The process of grantmaking can be lots of fun; however, with the fun come responsibilities.

 What sorts of responsibilities can there be, giving money away?

Grantmakers cannot give money to just anyone, particularly if their giving circle is part of a tax-exempt charity. They have to make sure that their giving falls within the rules of the Internal Revenue Service. And since they are giving money that technically does not solely belong to them, they want to make sure that their money will be spent wisely and by good stewards.

 Are these the reasons why calls for proposals sometimes look so daunting?

Yes, the calls must meet certain federal requirements as well as any other institutions to which the giving circle or philanthropy report. So in addition to meeting these requirements, the calls for proposals must be written in such a way that each applicant answers the same questions in a similar manner. That way, the grantmakers can evaluate all of the calls from a level playing field.

2

✳

Finding a Solution for Your Practice Pet Peeve

Do you:

Have a practice or education pet peeve that irritates you personally or that interferes with quality of care or other types of effectiveness or efficiency?

Have a mental picture of what it would look like if you were able to eliminate your pet peeve?

Believe that you have the energy and stamina to find a solution to your pet peeve?

Possess skills in bringing together other stakeholders who may share your concerns and be willing to be part of a project to solve the problem?

Know how to conduct a needs assessment and a literature review or find someone who can assist with these tasks?

Write well enough to articulate your ideas into a short concept paper that outlines how you would resolve the problem or find someone who will help with the writing exercise?

Glossary

Collaboration: A process by which individuals with differing perspectives on a problem agree to work together on solutions.

Concept paper: A brief overview of a subject.

Literature ("lit") review: A process of reading, analyzing, evaluating, and summarizing scholarly materials about a specific topic.

Needs assessment: A process for gathering information about current conditions within a population that underlie the need for an intervention. Usually forms the basis for an intervention plan.

Regardless of your work setting, whether it is inpatient or outpatient, public health or nursing education, you probably have noted practices that seem to bear little or no relation to outcomes and/or waste your time and energy. You can (1) develop work-arounds to bypass the problem, (2) whine, (3) acquiesce and give in to the practice, (4) quit, or (5) figure out how to change the practice to eliminate the problem. Grantwriting is a tool that you can use for the fifth strategy. Finding funds to help test or evaluate an alternative is certainly one way to provide attention and resources to the solution.

Even if you decide not to apply for a grant, the process involved in coming to a solution to your pet peeve is very similar to work you will need to do to resolve the problem. This chapter outlines a series of steps that will help you determine if and how to solve the problem. These steps include working with and through others to clarify the nature of the problem and possible solutions, finding out how others have solved this or similar problems, and sharpening your thoughts by developing a brief concept paper. If you follow the steps in this chapter, you will be ready to find money to support your solution.

"I don't have pet peeves, I have whole kennels of irritation."

—Whoopi Goldberg, comedian and actress

Converting your pet peeve into an actionable project (item)

"The secret is to gang up on the problem, rather than each other."

—Thomas Stallkamp, management consultant

Why should you work with and through others on your pet peeve?

Starting out, it's a good idea to determine that you are not alone in identification of your practice pet peeve. If your colleagues do not agree with your assessment of the practice as a pet peeve, then one of the other approaches mentioned above might be preferable to a full-blown, planned change project. In this first step, your goal is to acquire initial support for further investigation of possible solutions. Here are some steps you can take:

> **TIP** Make sure you feel so strongly about your pet peeve that you want to invest time, energy, and sweat equity to fix it.

* Talk informally with your peers about the issue. Do they feel the same way? What do they think is the problem? Do they have some solutions to offer?

* Frame the problem as one that has an impact on the work you do—either excessive time and effort or potential negative impact on quality, safety, cost; or in education, an impact on educational outcomes. This step is very important, because the next step, going to your supervisor, must be framed in words that are important to him or her. Otherwise, you might be seen as whining.

* Discuss the situation with your supervisor or manager. Your goal is to get initial approval to move forward on seeking

solutions. The key here is to sell your position sufficiently so that your manager will approve your delving into possible solutions. You want your manager on your side.

"Alone we can do so little; together we can do so much."

–Helen Keller, author, lecturer, and political activist

How do you energize others in solving your pet peeve?

Assuming that your manager agrees that you have a legitimate concern over which you have some control in solving, find others who are willing to help in a brainstorming process to be certain that the problem is clearly identified and that any possible resolutions will, in fact, lead to solving the problem. You should involve others in one or more meetings to ascertain that the problem is what it is and not something else and that possible solutions are within your purview and control. Make certain that all have the opportunity to participate and that their sentiments are, in fact, consistent with yours. Do not force your pet peeve on others.

TIP

Involve others early and often in this work.

Ways to achieve agreement or consensus on problem identification include holding a brainstorming session at a staff meeting or similar venue or using an electronic discussion board or e-survey.

At the completion of this phase, you should have one or two paragraphs written that describe the problem, the nature of the problem, its causes, and a list of possible solutions.

Finding out what others have done to solve the problem

"If you want to know the taste of a pear, you must change the pear by eating it yourself. If you want to know the theory and methods of revolution, you must take part in revolution. All genuine knowledge originates in direct experience."

—Mao Zedong, communist revolutionary

Why should you conduct a needs assessment, and how "scientific" does it need to be?

Conducting a needs assessment is an essential part of determining how much of a priority your team should place on solving the problem. Needs assessments help determine how prevalent the problem is or if it is just your own pet peeve. Needs assessments can be informal, meaning that you ask around and find out how many people have had this problem before, or they can be more formal. In the latter category, you may want to query others throughout your department, institution, or agency to determine if they have had the same problem, how often, and how the problem has been solved. You could use an electronic survey to find out the severity of the problem. In that case, you'd have to develop a survey and determine how to disseminate it throughout the agency. If your problem has actual data to support the need, such as patient falls or student grades, you should access these data

TIP Watch out for "groupthink" while you are getting buy-in for solving what should, by now, be everyone's pet peeve.

> **TIP** You must find out how extensive the problem is. Conducting a needs assessment, no matter how formal or informal, is essential.

during a certain time frame and form your opinions on the severity of the problem based on these data.

If you decide to seek grant funds to help resolve the problem, conducting a needs assessment, no matter how formal or informal it is, is essential. The grantor will want to know if their money is being invested in resolving a problem that is quantifiable.

Why and how should you conduct a literature review?

Conducting a literature (abbreviated "lit") review is always a good idea and, like the needs assessment, is critical toward establishing the importance of your problem and its possible solutions. Your goal by the end of this phase is to possess a compilation of research that has been published on the subject. Wait until you have more consensus on the problem and have involved others in the process before spending your valuable time on Google searches and other research approaches.

Literature reviews are important because they help further define and clarify problems, summarize previous investigations, identify relations, contradictions, gaps, and inconsistencies in studies, and suggest next steps (American Psychological Association, 2010). Begin by identifying the "key words" that are associated with your pet peeve. For example, if you are a nurse educator who believes that clinical evaluation of students in your project is too subjective, you might begin with a list of key words that includes "clinical evaluation," "clinical performance," "clinical evaluation software," and "nursing student assessment." Your hospital or university librarian will come in handy if you haven't conducted a literature review in awhile. Here are just a few pointers:

* Be organized. Remember the key words that you have identified and use those. However, you may find other key words that appear to be germane; don't eliminate them out of hand.

* Divide what you read between what is known and what is not known.

* Identify gaps or areas of controversy.

* Use appropriate databases or search tools. These may include search sites for education, health care, and nursing practice. See Box 2.1 for a description of three common search databases.

TIP Find out how others have identified the problem and the solutions they have tested. You don't want to reinvent the wheel, and you may indeed find that your proposal strikes new ground.

Remember, your primary goal in the lit review phase is to come up with a verification that you are not alone in the problem you have identified, meaning that others have worked on this same issue, and have tried various approaches to solving it.

Focusing on solutions

"I do not like to write—I like to have written."

–Gloria Steinem

Why should you write a "concept paper"?

And so finally, you have determined that your pet peeve is one that is shared among others, that it has an impact on the quality of the services you provide, and that others outside your sphere have also identified this problem and have worked on ways to resolve it. Now you are ready to put pen to paper and write a brief concept paper about the problem and its resolution. Concept papers serve at least two purposes. First, they help to focus your thinking on the topic and second, they can serve as a means for finding a potential funder.

This section provides a concise overview of writing concept papers. You can obtain more information on writing concept papers by consulting the sources in Box 2.2.

Concept paper writing is designed to help you accomplish the following. It:

* Crystallizes your thinking and forces you to communicate succinctly.

* Presents a case for resolving the problem to others, thus determining the level of external interest in helping reach resolution, and most importantly for the purposes of this book.

* Forms the basis for a proposal for funds.

(2.1) Internet links to writing concept papers

http://essayplant.com/conceptpaperwriting.php — This site contains a nice primer on concept paper writing. Simple to understand.

http://marthabianco.com/Courses/Cities/concept.html — Academic in nature. Begins with the research process (including a rather convoluted schema on the process of research). The information on writing a concept paper is found under number 5. Useful if you want more information on how the concept paper integrates into the research process, apart from grantwriting.

http://www.uml.edu/centers/cfwc/Community_Tips/Grant_Writing/Concept_Paper.html — A one-pager on how to write a one-pager. The author, Beata Murrell, also includes a link on how to succeed at grantwriting by doing thorough background research.

(2.2) Checklist for concept paper

☐   Introduction. In one or two paragraphs, describe the background leading to the problem. Set the problem within the context of the environment (academic, care setting, care delivery, and so forth).

☐   Statement of the problem. In one or two paragraphs, describe the problem, its causes, and the target population. Includes a brief description of the needs assessment to confirm the existence of the problem.

☐   Review of the literature. Briefly describes major work that has been conducted in this area with emphasis on work that documents solutions to the problem.

☐   Strategies for resolution of the problem. Describes the steps you propose to take to solve the problem, the timeline for resolution, and responsible persons.

☐   Outcome evaluation. Briefly states how you would measure effectiveness of your strategies in resolving the problem.

☐   Additional requirements by potential grantors, such as margins, font, and spacing specifications.

How should you write the concept paper?

The concept paper should be no more than two to three pages (single-spaced, 12-point font, 1-inch margins). Consult Box 2.2 for the component parts of the concept paper. Start by writing each heading and what should be contained in the section. Then write the section. Once you've written your first draft, make

TIP

Hone your thoughts and findings into a well-oiled concept paper that is succinct and to the point. It will make the case for your pursuing grantors to help resolve the problem.

sure that you have addressed each component part and have your collaborators critically review the draft. You want to ascertain that you have appropriately identified the problem and made a case for testing your solution.

Box 2.2 contains a checklist that helps you determine whether you've met all the requirements. Once you have completed your concept paper, you are ready to find someone who is willing to pay for your strategies for resolution. That is the subject of the next chapter.

TAKE-AWAY TIPS

✓ If you have a pet peeve, it's likely that others share your pain.

✓ Problem identification and resolution is a team sport. Find others to join your team.

✓ Use your organizational skills to bring your team together.

✓ Focus on identifying the problem by brainstorming or other team strategies.

✓ Find out how pervasive your problem is by conducting a needs assessment and analyzing the literature.

✓ Divide up the work among your team members.

✓ Write or participate in writing a concept paper that you will use to seek financial support to solve your pet peeve.

FAQs

Do all ideas for grant funding come from pet peeves?

No. Some people look for sources of funds without any specific pet peeves in mind. These people either get paid for doing this or they like to write grants and bring in money to their agency. For the average nurse who is seeking to take his or her first forays into grantwriting, it helps to be energized about something. It's sort of like writing a thesis or a long term paper—it helps to like the subject (or be irritated by it).

Why the focus on working with others?

Writing grants can be a team sport. Some people do it alone, but it's a lonely place to be. Working with others helps by doing the following: (1) spreads the responsibility for doing the work among multiple interested parties; (2) taps into the knowledge base and potential sources of funds or other contributions if you decide to look for funding; (3) looks good on others' job performance evaluations.

Do you *have* to conduct a needs assessment to determine the extent of the problem?

No. But it's not likely that you'll be funded without doing so. Grantors like to know that they are funding a worthy project. And how do you know that if you don't know the extent of the problem? This doesn't have to be a formal survey of the entire population. But it does have to reflect that you have looked into whether others believe that you have identified a gap that needs to be narrowed or eliminated.

Do you *have* to conduct a literature review?

No. But again, it's unlikely that you'll receive funding without a lit review. Without a literature review, how will you know that you have identified the problem adequately? That others have also identified the same issue? That others have attempted various solutions with varying degrees of success?

Do you *have* to write a concept paper?

Yes. Concept papers help you narrow your focus, provide discipline to the creative and critical thinking that you have put into your problem identification, and indicate to potential grantors that you are serious about finding a solution to your pet peeve.

References

American Psychological Association. (2010). *Publication manual of the American Psychological Association*(6th ed.). Washington, DC: Author.

3

✳

Searching for Money

Do you:

Know where the grantmakers are in your community?

Know if your agency funds projects?

Want to know more about state and federal funding of nursing and health-related projects?

Possess the skills to connect with grantmakers and other stakeholders associated with funding?

Know how to ascertain grantmakers' missions and funding priorities?

Know if your organization can be a recipient of grant funds?

With concept paper in hand and several partners willing to assist in the hunt for funds, you are now in a position to match your project with the priorities of grantmakers. This process takes time, but it is time well spent because you will make connections that will serve you and your projects well into the future. This chapter provides steps to accomplish the task; however, this process will be mostly about relationship building. As we discussed in Chapter 1, grant-makers are passionate about their investments, and they want to be assured that they are spending money wisely. Your role will be to convince them that investing in your project will promote their mission as well as helping you solve an identified problem. At the completion of this chapter, you should be equipped to begin your search for grantmakers and develop relationships that you can sustain well beyond your current project.

This chapter should unlock the mysteries and myths surrounding grantseeking. When most of us started down the path of grant-seeking, we wrung our collective hands on how to find people who would be willing to invest their money into our work. Sometimes this hurdle became so insurmountable in our minds that we scuttled our dreams and decided to work with the status quo or make the changes without additional funds. However, if you turn back to Chapter 1, you'll note that grantmakers are basically people like you—they possess funds over which they must, by law, be good stewards, and they follow their own rules about what their funds can be used for and how much they are willing to invest in work congruent with their mission and vision. So the trick for you is to find these people, make certain that their mission and vision is congruent with what you want to accomplish, and then court them.

That said, you might ask where these people are. Categorically, we can divide them into local funders, including your own agency; regional and state-based funders, including state government; and national funders, again, including federal government. Let's peel the onion.

Glossary

> **Key words:** Words or phrases the use of which in a call for proposals takes on a level of priority. These words or phrases may appear in **bold** or *italics* or may be used frequently in the funders' materials or proposal.

Nonprofit tax status: Not subject to taxation. In grantmaking, includes organizations exempt from taxes under the IRS code 501(c)(3); public schools, colleges, and universities; and other state and local governmental agencies.

Finding funders

"No idea is so outlandish that it should not be considered with a searching but at the same time a steady eye."

—Winston Churchill

Who is your organizational gatekeeper?

Assuming that you have never written a grant proposal before, you probably should start locally and/or regionally. The process of seeking and obtaining grant funds is similar regardless of where you start; however, the process can be less daunting when you work within your region of comfort. Having gained success, you can easily translate your skills to a larger venue. But starting locally is not a requirement, especially if you find in your search that there are no local or regional grantmakers investing in your type of project.

The search has two components. First, identify the person in your organization who is in charge of grantwriting, grantseeking, or fund development. That person is wired into the grantmaking community and should be able to offer suggestions, including names of contacts, types of grantmaking projects, and other information that will be useful.

Second, your institutional fund developer may also be the gatekeeper for any grant solicitations in your agency. So getting to know that person is essential. And staying on that person's good side is critical.

TIP

When you begin your search for funds, remember that there is probably someone in your agency whose job consists of fund development. Seek this person's advice early and often. Do not attempt to sidestep your agency fund developer.

Therefore, use your best manners when meeting and working with that person: (1) making and keeping appointments on time; (2) coming prepared with questions and ideas; (3) following up on suggestions and reporting back; (4) offering praise and thanks on a regular basis; (5) sending frequent updates via e-mail or other means.

Enter political savvy. As in all organizations, politics are overt and covert. Ideally the "grants" person in your agency should be helpful, intelligent, and encouraging of potential grantseekers. But we don't live in an ideal world. Make sure you understand (from others) how the grants person interacts with others, what makes him or her tick, and how to work most effectively with this person.

Should you talk with people in your community who have received grants from any source?

Sometimes you learn a lot from talking with others who have received grants. Find out who in your agency is working on a grant-funded initiative, whether it be in nursing or another discipline. Ask around in your professional network for others who may be involved in grant work. Make an appointment to visit with them. Usually they will be quite willing to discuss their project, how they got funded, and any other issue that you want to address. Box 3.1 contains a list of questions you might want to ask these grantees.

(3.1) Questions to ask grantees

* Why did you apply for a grant from XYZ Foundation? Did you approach them with your idea for funding, or did you respond to a call for proposals?

* With whom have you worked at the Foundation?

* What level of technical assistance did they provide while you were developing your proposal? Were they willing to read your drafts? Did they provide suggestions for how to improve your proposal?

Who are the local grantmakers, and where do you find them?

Do your homework early by learning who funds health and/or education grants in your community. Use at least three approaches, in addition to asking others about local foundations. Boxes 3.2 and 3.3 summarize steps for finding local grantmakers and sources of useful search information on finding national, regional, and local funders.

(3.2) Steps to finding local grantmakers

* Search the Internet for local funders.

* Isolate health and/or education, depending upon your problem area

* Browse grantmakers' websites, searching for the following:

    * Mission. Search for words that are consistent with your intended project.

    * Board of directors. Do you know any of these people, or do you know people who know them?

    * Foundation staff. See comments above for board of directors.

    * Look at the grantmakers' annual report and/or income tax returns, which are sometimes posted online. Search for key words congruent with your project, as well as amounts invested in funded projects.

(33) Steps to finding local grantmakers

Other useful Internet sources:

* Foundation Center (www.foundationcenter.org). Especially useful for examining tax records. Search for the IRS Form 990.
* GuideStar (www.guidestar.org). Provides information on charitable giving.

First, an Internet search will provide you with good information on local foundations, using "foundation" and your city and state as the key search words. Scroll through the list and make note of any that fund health and/or education endeavors. Search their individual websites, read what they fund, look at their income tax returns, and find the names of key staffers (president/CEO and project officers) and board members. Ask around and see if anyone you know knows any of the individuals on local foundations that look promising. You might also check out the Foundation Center (foundationcenter.org). This site offers detailed information on grantmakers—for a fee. Your public library or organization's library may already have a subscription to this service, and if so, use it. You'll be able to access the IRS Form 990—required of all tax-exempt organizations annually—for more information on the giving practices of the foundation (Foundation Center, n.d.).

Second, register and use the invaluable resources found at GuideStar.org. GuideStar is an organization with IRS tax-exempt status as a 501(c)(3). Its mission is "providing information that advances transparency, enables users to make better decisions, and encourages charitable giving" (home page). Once you have found potential funders, you can search their basic information on GuideStar at no charge. The site will confirm potential funders' tax status as well as the focus of their grantmaking (GuideStar, n.d.).

Third, find your local community foundation. You may locate this foundation through an Internet search or by visiting the Community Foundations website (www.communityfoundations.net). Community foundations are local organizations designed to pool together funds from endowments, grants, and other sources. Guided by local boards of trustees and staff, community foundations possess a keen interest and knowledge of local issues, opportunities, and resources to shape the community. They play key roles in solving community problems. They also provide education and resources for other local nonprofit leadership and maintain close ties with other grantors/funders in your community. They may help you identify potential sources of grant funds within your own community.

How do you find other funders outside of your community who invest in your community?

Use the same search tools to identify other potential grantors/ funders outside your local community. This process can seem intimidating because these funders are more geographically distant and larger. But there can be motivation in searching for sources at the state, national, or international level. Larger funding sources offer the possibility of more significant grant awards. In the following paragraphs you will find help with identifying sources of funding at the state and federal levels, as well as national or regional philanthropic institutions.

The state government

State governments issue grants for work that is within their domains of interest, i.e., the public's health and education. Issuing grants is a cost-effective way for states to accomplish certain tasks in areas in which their agencies need additional expertise, or are interested in funding innovation.

At times the process of finding sources of state funds may be arcane, but usually with perseverance you will be able to access information. And as the saying goes, if you know one state, you know one state. For example, in Virginia, you may need to e-file as a vendor in order to access the state's procurement process for grant or contract work to be done. Or you may need to search on the state's executive branch websites in public health and higher education. Sometimes grant funding can be found in the state's budget by searching key words within the budget document. Do enroll in as many e-mail distribution lists as you can find through Internet searches of state websites.

After exhausting Internet sources for state funding opportunities, use the old-fashioned approach of talking with people who can help you access information about funding opportunities within the state. You're looking for the contact person in the state agency who administers grant funding for the project that is as close to what you're aiming to do. If you are in nursing education, start with the grants department at your institution and ask that person for their contacts within the state higher education community. If you are located in a health care setting and have no in-house grants expertise, use your professional network to find sources. This process sometimes takes awhile, but it can be most useful because you will meet people along the way. Make sure you keep their contact information because you never know when you might need them again. Remember, your overall focus is relationship building; show appreciation by acknowledging the assistance you receive along the way. Courtesy goes a long way to receiving support in the future.

The federal government

While we have 50 states, the District of Columbia, and assorted territories in the United States (not to mention international sources), and thus more than 50 varieties of state grant funding initiatives, we have only one federal government. Consequently, the federal resources are consolidated, but they can be somewhat convoluted and arcane as well. For nursing, nursing education, and nursing workforce funding sources, you will need to access the website for the Division of Nursing, Health and Human Resources (HRSA), which is part of the U.S. Department of Health and Human Services. Box 3.3 contains links to specific federal agencies that fund nursing projects.

You are probably reading this book because you are interested in stepping into the waters of grantseeking and grantwriting. The requirements for writing a federal grant proposal are beyond the parameters of this book; that said, grantwriting follows a similar process regardless of the size and complexity of the proposal

3 Searching for Money

requirements. Although you may not start your journey with a federal grant, now is the time to familiarize yourself with the federal grant opportunities. Sign up to receive electronic notifications of federal nursing grant projects. Use the links in Box 3.3 to help you with this. One note of caution: be careful of the number of requests you make for electronic notification. Try to be selective in your requests. These can be overwhelming in nature and number. You can always unsubscribe those that do not appear to be helpful.

Foundations with national and/or international focus

As with local funders, national foundations make grants in health and/or education to recipients across the United States (and sometimes internationally). Box 3.3 contains a listing of Internet sources for federal and national sources of grants. You will want to search each of their websites for the same type of information that you seek when looking at local funders, answering these questions:

* What is their mission?

* What are their current funding areas?

* What organizations have they funded recently?

* What are typical award amounts?

* Are there ongoing or new opportunities for funding?

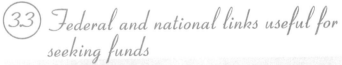

(3.3) *Federal and national links useful for seeking funds*

www.federalgrantswire.com — This site is a free resource for federal grants, but it is not a government-run site. You can search by federal agency, subject area, or use the Google search box where you can put in your key words to search for funding sources. Once you click on a subject, the site will take you to a description of the project, its status, grant objectives (read this carefully for key words), use of funds and funding restrictions, eligibility requirements, application procedures, and deadlines, with a hyperlink to the federal agency in charge of the grant project.

Federal agencies

http://www.grants.gov/search/category.do — Grants.gov is the website that lists all federal grant opportunities. On this selected page, you can search by category (education, environment, health) and obtain a listing of all open grant opportunities.

http://www.grants.gov/applicants/email_subscription.jsp — This page contains information on how to register for grants RSS feeds and grant updates and notices.

www.hrsa.gov — The Health Resources and Services Administration (HRSA) of the U.S. Department of Health and Human Services is the primary federal agency for access to health care services for people who are uninsured, isolated, or medically vulnerable. HRSA is composed of six bureaus and nine offices, all of which are described on the HRSA website. Of interest to nursing education are the following:

* The Bureau of Health Professions, which funds health professional training grants and health workforce studies.

* The Maternal and Child Bureau, which funds grants to improve health of mothers, children, and families. These grants may be administered through your state's public health department.

www.doleta.gov — The Employment and Training Administration of the U.S. Department of Labor is the agency that administers grants for job training and worker dislocation projects. Occasionally, grants are available to improve worker performance, such as conflict resolution in the work environment.

www.ahrq.gov/fund/ — The Agency for Healthcare Research and Quality funds projects focused on comparative effectiveness research, prevention and care management, value in health care (reducing inefficiencies and redundancies), health information technology, patient safety, and emerging/innovative issues.

continues

continued

National foundations

A Google search of "health foundations grants" will bring up pages of results. The major sites are listed below, but they are by no means exclusive. Check also on **www.tophealthgrants.com** to see a listing of recent and active grants.

www.rwjf.org — The Robert Wood Johnson Foundation is the nation's largest philanthropy devoted solely to the public's health. The Foundation has a rich history of funding nursing-related projects.

www.wkkf.org — The W.K. Kellogg Foundation funds health-related projects nationally and internationally focused on health, agriculture, and education.

http://www.uml.edu/centers/cfwc/Community_Tips/Grant_Writing/networking.html — This is a brief piece on networking to find funds. It contains a wonderful list of things to do when looking for and engaging partners in your venture.

At the completion of this stage of your search, you should have a list of local (state, federal, or national) funders who make grants in health or education. Now you are ready to move on to evaluate their grants, seeking information about the congruence between what they invest in and your area of interest.

TIP Find funders who are investing in your area of interest. Use Internet search engines, talk with resources, and review successful proposals.

Evaluating grantmakers' grants: Getting to know them

"It's all about relationships and who you know."

—Anonymous

This stage of the search for finding funds involves developing a real understanding of what the grantmakers deem important for their awards. When you are finished with this stage, you will possess a greater certainty that your idea is fundable, and you will have narrowed the possible sources of funding. It involves reading as much as possible about funders' grantmaking opportunities from their websites and other written materials, analyzing your own words and thoughts carefully for a match, communicating with funders for clarification, and sending your concept paper to funders for feedback.

Where do you start with finding the best fit for funding?

You start by analyzing the available grantmaking resources in your area. Let's use the following example.

You are the simulation laboratory instructor in a baccalaureate nursing education program housed within a state university that is not part of an academic health science system. In your lab, students work in scenarios that consist solely of nursing students and their instructors. You believe that student learning, especially in the area of interdisciplinary team communication, would be improved by including other health professionals in scenario work. To test this, you propose to invite community pharmacists, family practice physicians and nurse practitioners, and laboratory technicians to participate in selected scenarios. You seek grant funding for $5,000 for scenario development and evaluation, honoraria for community participants, and use of a standardized tool that measures interdisciplinary communication. Let's further suppose that you have worked with your colleagues in developing this idea, you have administrative support, and you've crafted a concept paper that describes the problem, proposed solution, and potential impact on improved patient care and staff collaboration. What's next?

You have done your search of regional foundations and have found the following:

* The Smith Foundation has recently awarded North Central University a grant to develop a state-of-the-art clinical practice simulation laboratory for training nursing and allied health students and providing opportunities for continuing professional education for licensed health professionals in the region.

* The Jones Foundation awarded Lake Hospital (in your community) with a grant to enhance its simulation laboratory using "new approaches to health and healthcare that make a difference and generate synergies that bring resources to add value and enhance outcomes."

* The Memorial Foundation funds health-related projects making a significant impact on the community, particularly those that address unmet health care needs. The foundation has four areas of emphasis, one of which is "nursing and other health education."

* The Health Foundation has three funding priorities: healthy lifestyles, mental health, and safety-net health care.

From your review of these four grantmakers, you determine that at least two of the four (Smith and Jones) specifically state "simulation" in their grant overviews. Memorial funds "nursing . . . education." The Health Foundation's priorities do not specifically relate to health professional education, but can they be ruled out? Here are some ways you can determine whether any or all of these foundations' funding initiatives are consistent with what you want to do.

How do you find the right grantmaker?

The key to successful proposal submission is understanding and articulating how your ideas for funding are consistent with the funder's mission and grant initiative. Getting there requires real work on your part, but the work has its rewards.

Conduct an environmental scan on the foundations

You will want to obtain as much information as possible about these funders. Read about them in press releases. Explore their websites. Look for their funding priorities and their grant awards. Find out who is on their boards and their staff. If they post their IRS Form 990 (required of all nonprofits), read the document.

Attend grantmakers' funding workshops

Some grantmakers, especially large foundations and the government, will hold workshop sessions as they announce new funding opportunities. If at all possible, you should attend the sessions. The knowledge you gain will be well worth the cost of travel to the workshop. If you are unable to travel, join in via conference call or webcast. Listen carefully for key words, or words that appear to be used frequently in their materials, on what they will be looking for in proposals. Usually they will offer their proposal evaluation criteria. Use these criteria while crafting your proposal, making absolutely certain that you use their key words and are cognizant of the weight assigned to each portion of the proposal.

Read successful proposals

Some grantmakers permit open access to successful proposals. You can learn much from reading these, including their use of key words consistent with the grantmakers' priorities, adherence to proposal writing guidelines, consistency between the written narrative and the budget, and so forth. As you read, compare your ideas with the funded proposals. Is there a level of congruency between what you are seeking and what has been funded? Will your idea build on the work that is being done by funded projects? Are there other leverage points that you might use in making a case for funding your idea?

Talk with grantees

Those who have received funding are usually more than willing to engage in a conversation about their projects, from idea generation through project award. They are also likely to talk about the challenges they have experienced along the way in their relationships with the grantmakers. Use these conversations to gain insight in how to engage with the funders.

Talk with the grantmakers

Usually you can find the appropriate person within the funding agency for a conversation. This person may be a project officer or an executive within the agency, depending on the size of the funder. Alternatively, if you know a board member or another person associated with the grantmaker, start there. The key to this approach is to create a relationship with the funders. As you read in Chapter 1, people who invest in ideas are very interested in making certain that their investment is well spent. Therefore, the more you engage these people in your ideas and thoughts, the more you will learn about them and most likely, the more you will learn about how to present your idea in the very best possible light.

Send them your concept paper

Send your paper after you have established a relationship with the funders. Do not send your paper without any dialog first. Why? Remember: To a certain extent, grant award making is an interpersonal process that includes learning about the funders, establishing a relationship, and "selling" your idea to the grantmaker. When you send your paper, ask for feedback on the merit

TIP Use a multi-focal process for learning about possible funders. This includes environmental scanning and establishing a relationship with those who have received funds and the funders themselves.

of your idea, whether it fits into their funding priorities, and suggestions for improvement.

Oops. Can your organization receive grant funds?

"Mistakes are the portals of discovery."

–James Joyce

One last word before we move on to the next phase in our work. Suppose you find yourself in a situation where you learn that your agency is not eligible to receive funds from a foundation. This is one of those pesky situations in which grantseekers sometimes find themselves.

What types of agencies are able to receive grant funding?

The vast majority of grants are issued to tax-exempt organizations. These include:

* A tax-exempt organization described in Section 501(c)(3) of the Internal Revenue Code

* State and local government agencies

* Public colleges and universities

In the event that your agency does not qualify to receive grant funding, what alternatives do you have?

Don't throw in the towel. You have several options. First, find out if your agency has a tax-exempt foundation or charitable arm. If so, you can ask if that agency would serve as the fiscal agent for your project. Second, partner with someone who is interested in your project and is an employee of one of the tax-exempt agencies listed on page 40. The fiscal agent for your project would then reside in another agency from your own. In Chapter 2, we discussed the importance of forming a team that includes others who may share the same nursing practice pet peeve. If your team includes representatives of agencies eligible to apply for grant funding, this would be a perfect opportunity to strengthen the collaboration. Your collaborator would be more than the fiscal agent; he or she would be an active participant in the grant process, working to solve the project while serving as the fiscal agent.

TIP If your agency cannot accept grants, find a partner who can accept grants and ask them to become the fiscal agent for your proposal and to be an active participant in the funded project.

TAKE-AWAY TIPS

✓ Searching for money is like hunting and gathering. You have to know the spots where the funds can be found, and you spend time toiling to yield the harvest of funds to support your project. So be systematic and perseverant.

✓ Searching for money is also all about acquiring, building, and nurturing relationships with organizational gatekeepers and grantmakers. Mind your manners and don't hesitate to ask for assistance and feedback.

✓ Use the Internet and other professional and community connections to find potential grantmakers. If you are overwhelmed, ask someone with experience in grantseeking to help you.

✓ Use every opportunity at your disposal to find grantmakers and learn their priorities. This includes attending workshops, reading successful proposals, and asking for technical assistance.

✓ Make sure that your agency can receive grant funds according to tax law. If not, fall back to Plan B and find an agency that can accept funds to be your fiscal agent.

FAQs

 You describe much of searching for funds as being interpersonal in nature. Can't I just send out my concept paper to all the sources of funds in my area and see who responds?

Yes, you can do that, but it's not a good idea. Most if not all the sources will hit the delete button before responding to your "cold call." Take time to develop the relationships and learn about possible grantmakers.

 Suppose I develop a good relationship with a grant-maker, and I still am unable to interest him/her in my project. Why would this happen?

Most likely your project does not fit the mission of the grant-maker. Read the mission statement and learn about the projects the grantmaker has funded. If yours doesn't "fit," then move on. However, use good manners and never show disrespect for a grantmaker, even if he or she is not interested. You never know when you will have an idea that the grantmaker will be interested in. Don't burn bridges, ever, with foundations.

 You write primarily about local foundations. Should I ignore or not seek funds from the state or federal government or a national foundation?

By all means, consider all sources of funds. If you're just start-ing out, local funders are more likely to work with you, and that is important. Usually, local funders' requests for propos-als are less intense and convoluted in nature, and you may be more comfortable establishing a relationship with a member of the community. The process of finding interested funders is the same, regardless of whether you are going local or national, government or private. Get some success under your belt with a small grant from a local funder (even your own agency) first, before going for a larger grant. Starting with smaller, local funders also has the advantage of helping you build a portfolio of success. Larger funders take into consideration your experience with managing awards and projects.

 You didn't finish the example given in the chapter about seeking funds to support a collaboration-building simulation scenario. What is the answer?

There is no answer to this question. Most likely the person seeking the funds would be able to interest three of the four foundations listed, but all four could be possible candidates. Success would all depend upon how the project is packaged (for the foundation) and the relationships that were built between the fund-seeker and the fund-giver.

4

✳

Project Planning

Do you:

Know others who will help you write a proposal that will resolve the problem you have identified?

Possess the skills to recruit these people?

Possess the skills to identify the problem and come to consensus with your team?

Know how to use a logic model template to achieve a workable plan to resolve the problem?

At this point, you have an idea that you believe will help solve a problem; you have completed some preliminary work on this problem, including clarification of the problem and achieving consensus among your colleagues that you are not alone. You have also searched the literature to examine what others have done to solve the problem and sought information on its prevalence. You have written a concept paper. And finally, you've sent your paper to funders to determine their interest. Best of all, you have found some possible sources of funds, and now you are preparing to write your proposal. In this chapter, we'll describe how you go about putting flesh on the bones of your concept paper, readying it for the larger proposal submission. This involves developing your project to the point where it is ready to describe more fully and to have financial and other resources attached to the project components. By the end of this chapter, you'll have the tools to accomplish this.

Glossary

Activities, a.k.a. action steps: Each of the project steps planned in conducting the project. Each step is one part of a series of steps toward achieving a certain outcome. Some activities will also produce outputs (W. K. Kellogg Foundation, 2006).

Assumptions: Beliefs we have about the project, the people involved, and the context and the way we think the project will work (W. K. Kellogg Foundation, 2006). Assumptions form the foundation or are the preconditions existing before beginning a change project.

External factors: Environment in which the project exists. Includes a variety of external factors that interact with and influence project action. External factors are more likely than not variables over which you have no or little control.

Goal, a.k.a. objective, or long-term objective, or impact: The intended aim or impact over the life of the project. For each action in a project, you should answer the question, "How will this affect the goal we are trying to achieve?"

Impact: The desired endpoint of the project. See "goal."

Inputs, a.k.a. resources: Resources, contributions, and investments that comprise the means by which a project is achieved.

Logic model: Systematic and visual way to present and share one's understanding of the relationships among resources used to operate a project, activities planned, and changes or intended results. Displays the sequence of actions that describe what a project is and will do: how investments link to results. The logic model has five core components: inputs, outputs, outcomes, assumptions, and external factors (W. K. Kellogg Foundation, 2006).

Outcomes, a.k.a. objectives: In some models, objectives are identified as short-term, intermediate, and long-term outcomes. Results or changes for individuals, groups, communities, organizations, or systems (W. K. Kellogg Foundation, 2006). The changes expected to result from a project—changes among clients, communities, systems, or organizations.

Outputs, a.k.a. deliverables: Activities, services, events, and products that reach people who participate in the project or who are targeted. These are usually quantifiable. For example, how many participants attended a workshop, what materials were developed in the course of the project, were minutes kept of project meetings?

Problem statement, a.k.a. issue statement or situation: A description of the problem that the project seeks to solve.

Series of "if-then" relationships: The relationships that connect the components of the logic model: *if* resources are available to the project, *then* project activities can be implemented; *if* project activities are implemented successfully, *then* certain outputs and outcomes can be expected; *if* the project achieves the desired outcomes, *then* it will accomplish the intended impact on the targeted population.

SMART: Acronym used as qualifiers for writing outcomes (objectives) and impacts (goals): Specific * Measurable * Action-oriented * Realistic * Timed (ChangingMinds.org; nd).

Convene a planning team

"None of us is as smart as all of us."

–Ken Blanchard, management expert

Who should be on the team?

It is time to convene your team. Proposal writing is a team sport, especially for the novice. It's like putting together a puzzle where you know what the final product will look like, but in the meantime you start out with hundreds of seemingly disparate pieces. Teams bring together people with varied skills and perspectives, and these are invaluable contributions to the effort. Whom shall you invite? Here are some ideas.

Cast a large enough net to catch the skills you need. Consider colleagues who:

* Are experts in the problem you want to solve.

* Are systems thinkers who can see multiple perspectives on the problem and its resolution.

* Communicate well in writing.

* Are willing to invest some time in your project without remuneration.

⁕ Have participated in proposal writing. This competency may be the most important selection criterion if this is your first proposal-writing experience. But not having an experienced person to join your team should not be a deal breaker; it just complicates the task at hand.

⁕ Represent "knowledge" interests. These might be collaborative partners who bring academic expertise such as local university faculty, experts from other relevant agencies or other professionals in a field closely related to your project focus.

⁕ Represent "moneyed" interests. That is, include people who would be willing to invest in this project as you seek funding. Read more about this in Chapter 5 under the heading "What should you write about sustainability?"

How do you get people on your team?

Be prepared to "sell" your "ask" to the potential team members. What will they get in return for helping you?

⁕ A bullet point on their curriculum vitae or résumé?

⁕ The opportunity to work with other creative thinkers in solving a problem that needs fixing?

⁕ A potential commitment to participate in this project, should it be funded?

⁕ A share of funding that may benefit their agency or specific position?

⁕ A mentoring opportunity?

Some individuals will participate for any or all of the reasons you offer. They understand the value of mentoring, being an active participant in problem solving, and perhaps playing a role in a funded project. A team of five individuals contributing to a proposal development means that each person writes only a portion of the proposal and not the whole document. This is sometimes the best selling point.

What roles do team members play, including you?

Remember that teams need a coach and players. You may turn out to be the coach, or you may ask another more experienced person to serve in that role. Each team member must figure out his or her role and level of contribution. Consequently, early on, you should all understand the parameters of the task and be held to timelines as closely as possible. Remember, if team members' participation is not part of their job description, you must be willing to accept less than total commitment, especially from those who volunteer their time to the effort. Do not be discouraged.

TIP Bring together a team to help with writing the proposal. Members should complement your competencies and skills and be willing to contribute to the overall effort.

Achieve consensus on the problem

"You've got to be very careful if you don't know where you are going, because you might not get there."

–Yogi Berra, professional athlete

What steps are involved with problem identification and consensus?

The team should agree early on a clear statement of the problem. This seems like a no-brainer, but as teams are composed of individual players, all must possess a common understanding of the nature of the work to be done, including a statement of the goal. That said, start your team discussion with the endpoint. How will it look if the problem is solved? Will cancer patients experience end-of-life care that is tailored to their preferences? Will you be able to determine which types of dressings promote healing and comfort and prevent superficial infection among cardiac surgical patients? Will expedited partner therapy be associated with a decrease in the incidence of STDs among your client population? Will you determine which type of simulation training is associated with increased confidence and knowledge levels of nursing students studying maternal-child health nursing?

Once you have agreed on the goal, revisit the problem statement. Do all team members have a clear understanding of the problem? Do they agree that the problem is, in fact, a problem and not a symptom of a bigger problem? You may decide to write a series of if-then or declarative statements that will help to clarify the problem. Here are several examples:

* The use of the XYZ assessment tool to measure patient wishes and values will be associated with improved patient experiences in end-of-life care.

* Cardiac surgical patients who are exposed to the use of XYZ dressing will experience more rapid healing with less discomfort and reduced superficial infection rates than cardiac surgical patients who are not exposed to XYZ dressings.

* If senior nursing students receive XYZ simulation experiences, they will demonstrate more confidence and knowledge of care of maternal-child patients than senior nursing students receiving traditional classroom learning.

* The use of expedited partner therapy for STD treatment will be associated with a decrease in incidence and/or recurrence of STDs among clinic patients.

What roles do the needs assessment and literature review play in establishing the problem and its resolution?

Part of this problem clarification stage should be to examine carefully the evidence of the magnitude of the problem. This includes two steps: (1) conducting a needs assessment and (2) performing a literature search. Your team should do both, if you have not already done so.

The needs assessment consists of an analysis of the prevalence of the problem. How do you determine the prevalence? You may:

* Conduct a survey. Explain what you have determined as the problem and ask others if they have experienced the same problem. Do this with an electronic or paper-and-pencil survey or conduct interviews.

* Conduct a chart or documentation review. How many times has the problem been identified in the past few months? In the past year?

TIP Make sure that you have defined the problem, have determined the need for resolution, and have documented the means by which others have worked to resolve the problem.

The needs assessment does not have to be a highly technical process, but it does have to accomplish at least two objectives. First, it has to validate that the problem exists enough to warrant a solution. Second, it has to demonstrate to your grantmakers that you have determined that there is a problem for which their funds will contribute to a resolution.

The second phase of determining the prevalence of this problem is to conduct a literature review. You may have conducted a preliminary review in developing your concept paper. Now it is time for your team to use its skills in digging a bit deeper to search for further written documentation of work that has been conducted in this problem area. At the completion of the search, you will have determined that:

* You are not alone; others have identified the problem and have worked on its resolution.

* The problem has a common set of attributes identified in the literature.

* Resolutions have achieved varying degrees of success.

* Your ideas for resolution may add to the body of literature about the problem and means to resolve it.

Develop the plan for problem resolution

"Again and again, the impossible decision is solved when we see that the problem is only a tough decision waiting to be made."

—Dr. Robert Schuller, televangelist

How does a logic model assist in problem resolution?

The next phase of work for your planning team will be to agree on how to solve the problem. Using a logic model can serve as the template for problem resolution. Once completed, the logic model depicts the problem, your intended outcomes, the approaches you will use to achieve your outcomes, who will be responsible for the strategies, what resources will be needed, and what external factors may serve as barriers and facilitators toward problem resolution (Kellogg Foundation, 2004). Consult Box 4.1 for a logic model template and Figure 4.1 for an example of the logic model based on the example described in the template.

4.1 Logic model example

Pain management improvement is a project designed to engage the nursing staff in implementing a pain assessment protocol that improves the identification and management of pain in all patients in our agency. The theory of change for this project is based on these assumptions: (1) Nurses want to provide the best care for their patients tailored to the patients' involvement in their care; (2) the agency desires to improve patient care and satisfaction. This theory of change is reflected in the upper part of the logic model below.

Project Logic Model

Inputs	Activities	Outputs	Outcomes	Impact
Stakeholders, such as nurse managers, staff developers, staff nurses, and patients; information technology support; and agency policies.	Conduct a search of the pain assessment literature and research. Evaluate pain assessment tools for the evidence of their effectiveness. Select tools that meet an evidence threshold and are age- and condition-appropriate.	Compendium of pain assessment tools with evidence base for each and applicability for age groups and patient conditions. Series of educational offerings for nurses describing the use and efficacy of assessment tools.	Nurses consistently utilize a standardized pain assessment tool according to established, evidence-based guidelines. Agency policies align with the use of a standardized pain assessment protocol.	Patient care can be improved by a reduction in pain through a carefully designed and executed program of pain management.

Inputs	Activities	Outputs	Outcomes	Impact
	Develop and implement a series of classes to educate nurses on the use of the tools.	Unit and agency policies amended for consistency with pain assessment tool standardization and utilization.	Patients report pain management strategies employed in a timely manner with corresponding reduction in pain.	
	Determine changes that need to be made in agency and evaluation policies.	Nurse evaluation tools consistent with standardized pain assessment utilization.		
	Review/revise processes for measuring patient pain and satisfaction with pain management.	Patient scores on pain assessment tools and follow-up interventions.		
		Patient scores on patient satisfaction surveys post-discharge.		

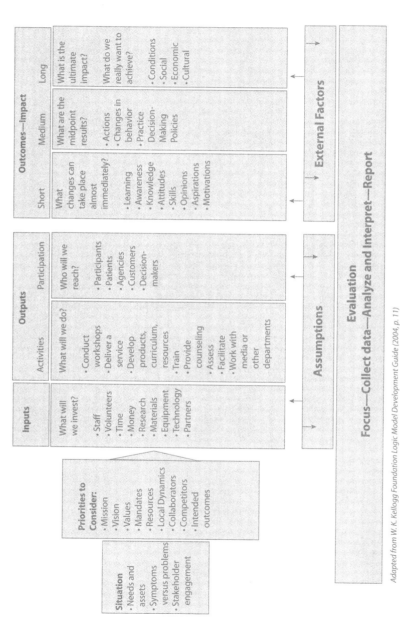

Figure 4.1   Project planning, implementation, and evaluation using a logic model

What are the components of the logic model?

The impact of your project is your end-state. Start with determining the impact by answering this question: *If your project is successful, what will be its impact?* Make sure you have described it as clearly as you can. Will patient care be improved due to a reduction in patients' pain? Will the educational program be enhanced because students score at or above a certain grade consistently? What will the overall impact be if this project is successful?

Next, describe the outcomes you hope to achieve. These are your overall project objectives or goals and should be stated declaratively using the action words that you hope to achieve. The question to be answered in writing your goals/outcomes is, *If we do all of these things, will we have achieved the impact we are seeking?* For example, in improving patient care by reducing pain, we could envision the outcomes that are identified in Box 4.1 regarding the use of a standardized pain assessment tool, development of agency policies, and patient reports of pain.

The next step is to enumerate the outputs that will measure whether you have achieved your outcomes. Outputs are the deliverables that you can document as you work toward achieving your goals/outcomes. In our pain management example, we listed several tangible outputs: compendium of pain assessment tools, series of educational offerings, policies, tools, and patient scores.

If we are going to achieve the desired impact and outcomes, we will need to design a series of activities aimed at outcome achievement. Our logic model could guide us to develop a series of activities that are included in the example. These include the actions that must be accomplished in order to achieve the outcomes.

And finally, using the logic model as a schema for project planning and implementation, we will need to include all the elements that must be considered before beginning our project and included throughout the project. These are the inputs or external factors. In our example, we included foundation funding; stakeholders, such as nurse managers, staff developers, staff nurses, and patients; information technology support; and agency policies. When you are planning your project, you want to list all the resources (human, fiscal) that will have an impact on the outcomes of the project. You should account for each in the planning of the project.

This stage of problem planning involves all members of the team pulling together their best thinking on how the project will roll out, once funded. At the completion of this stage, you will have a detailed project blueprint. Some funders require this level of detail; others do not. The more flesh you can put on the bones of your project in this phase, the better off you will be once the grantmakers approve you for funding.

What have you achieved if you have completed your logic model?

Think of the finished logic model as a completed jigsaw puzzle. When you start to work on the puzzle, you know the end state because you can see it on the puzzle box. Using the logic model analogy, the completed puzzle is the impact. Your team understands the impact and must agree on a set of outcomes, which in other problem resolution models are called objectives. Once you know your outcomes (or objectives) and impact, each member of the team can work on other parts of the logic model.

To extend the jigsaw puzzle analogy, one member may work on the corners and another on an interesting notable piece of the inside, while a third member tackles something else. You can divide the logic model up as well, with each member taking an objective to work on. For each outcome, a member develops a set of activities that, when completed, will achieve the stated outcomes. These activities will lead to a set of deliverables or outputs. The team will now have a model that consists of a series of activities designed to achieve expected outcomes, which taken as a whole, will solve the problem.

TIP Develop your plan for problem resolution so that you know what work will be done, by whom, when, and how you will document and measure its completion.

Your last step will be to examine your existing resources and determine the strengths or facilitators toward problem resolution as well as the barriers. These resources should include an analysis of the personnel and money needed to accomplish the problem resolution. Team members should acknowledge where the barriers might be and work on strategies to resolve them. Understanding where there are gaps between the resources available and those that are needed will help you inform funders about how a grant can be used to meet the project goals and objectives.

References

ChangingMinds.org. (n.d.). *SMART objectives*. Retrieved from http://changingminds.org/disciplines/hr/performance_management/smart_objectives.htm.

W. K. Kellogg Foundation. (2006). W. K. Kellogg Foundation Logic Model Development Guide. Retrieved from http://www.wkkf.org/knowledge-center/resources/2006/02/WK-Kellogg-Foundation-Logic-Model-Development-Guide.aspx.

TAKE-AWAY TIPS

✓ **Recruit a group of people to help you with project planning. Find those who will offer a different perspective and are committed to helping you with this project.**

✓ **Make sure that all agree on the problem and share the same meaning of key words.**

✓ **Encourage all team members to work to their capacity. Understand that varying degrees of contribution may be made by paid staff and volunteers; assign tasks accordingly. Be organized, keep meetings focused, and stick to the time allocated. No one likes disorganization.**

✓ **Make sure that your needs assessment quantifies that there is, in fact, a problem to resolve.**

✓ **Use your literature review to help inform strategies that you might be able to use in problem resolution.**

✓ **Use a logic model template to develop the parameters and particulars of the problem resolution.**

FAQs

You describe the logic model in a linear fashion, basically starting at the end (with the impact) and working in reverse. Does the project planning team have to work in that direction?

No, the beauty of the logic model is that, like working a jigsaw puzzle, you can put in pieces where you think they need to go. At some point, you will need to step back and analyze what is out of place and what is missing.

In working through problem resolution with a logic model, what must you absolutely know before you start?

Three things are essential in starting this process: (1) an agreement on the problem itself that needs to be resolved; (2) the ultimate impact if the problem is resolved; and (3) the objectives or outcomes that you hope to achieve.

Why should we use a team to do this?

More minds help inform the process. Everyone brings his or her own perspective and diversity to the situation, so that when the problem is identified, it is more likely to be one that others recognize as well and can see the value in resolving. The more hands and minds involved, the less work that needs to be done by each individual.

What if no one wants to help?

Don't give up hope until you have explored every option available to you, short of extortion, unless you have the ability to promise something that will benefit those who participate. If you still cannot find someone, you can try this by yourself, but going it alone makes the project much more difficult to execute.

Do I have to lead this effort?

It depends. If there is a better leader who is as motivated as you, perhaps this person will assume a leadership position.

 Do I have to use a logic model?

No. There are other ways to plan a problem resolution. Another common approach is to use a modified strategic planning approach. In this approach, you establish the goal, write objectives to achieve the goal, set out your actions to achieve each objective, and evaluate your success by determining what deliverables will be evidenced by the completion of each activity. This method is very similar to the logic model and uses some of the same terminology. It tends to be less of a systems approach, but it is utilitarian as well.

 This seems so time consuming. Is it necessary?

Well, yes, but it's not as time consuming as you think. By the time you've arrived at this stage, you have already thought about your problem quite a bit. You may or may not have developed your concept paper (this chapter can actually be implemented prior to developing a concept paper). The time-consuming part is engaging others in your effort. Once you have a team, you can create a logic model in about 4 hours.

5

✳

Making the "Ask" or Responding to a Request for Proposals

Do you:

Follow directions well?

Know how to determine if your agency is eligible to receive grant funds?

Know what to include in each section of a request or call for proposals?

Know how to weigh the relative merit of each part of the proposal according to the grantmaker's priorities?

In developing their request for proposals (RFPs) or call for proposals (CFPs), grantmakers indicate their requirements for grantseekers. The proposal developers are specific in their design and intent, and you should adhere to their requirements as closely as possible.

Following is a glossary of proposal components. While some proposals may vary in what they require, most will ask for the elements listed in the glossary. Let's examine each.

Glossary

Budget: How the applicant will spend the award. This usually consists of a table outlining the expense components, such as project staff, supplies, equipment, travel and meetings, and consultants/contracted personnel. In addition, this section may also require a budget narrative that explains how each of the expenses will contribute to the project goals and outcomes.

Eligibility criteria: Tax status of applicant agency requirements. Usually government or public entities and nonprofit organizations that are tax-exempt under Section 501(c)(3) of the Internal Revenue Code. The funder may place other requirements as well, such as location of the applicant, population demographics, poverty, rurality, type of educational program.

Letters of support: Documentation of agreement and participation from stakeholders, such as proposed project staff and partners, memoranda of understanding, letters from community leaders affirming need and capacity of your organization to manage a grant.

Purpose: The intent of the project. Examples: research to solve a clinical problem; an innovation project, such as testing a new strategy for smoking cessation; replication or expansion of a successful program using a different population or location; or development/implementation of educational content to meet a growing need.

Selection criteria: The items that must be included in the proposal.

Submission requirements: A description of the details for submission, such as length of the proposal, margins, font, spacing, and what can be included in an appendix.

Purpose

"To forget one's purpose is the commonest form of stupidity."

–Friedrich Nietzsche

What are the absolute requirements for the project purpose?

Your proposal request must match a grantor's purpose. This maxim sounds simple in theory but is not always so simple in practice. If you are seeking funds to support an educational innovation, make sure that the funder is supporting educational innovations. If you are uncertain about the funder's intent, call the funder and ask the question. For example, a funder may be allocating awards for nursing innovations, and your idea is a nursing education innovation. You will want to sell your idea as a means for improving nursing through educating students, and you will want to present your idea in that manner.

Be bold in making your "ask," but don't invest time in writing a proposal that doesn't match the funder's intent. If you are not successful at first, keep looking for a funder who will fund an educational innovation. Be sure to search outside the usual health-related foundations into educational foundations for support.

What are the components of the purpose in a CFP?

> **TIP**
>
> **Write your purpose succinctly, inclusively, and absolutely consistent with the grantmaker's intent for the funding opportunity.**

In writing your project's purpose, be sure to include these elements: the action, the target population, the intervention, and the setting. For example, here is a purpose statement:

To assess similarities and differences regarding end-of-life preferences between patients on the oncology and palliative care units and the perception of those preferences by their families and clinicians.

Eligibility criteria

"Hypocrisy is the essence of snobbery, but all snobbery is about the problem of belonging."

—Alexander Theroux, novelist

Who is eligible to receive a grant?

As described in Chapter 3, to receive a grant, your agency must belong to an exclusive club. The two types of entities that may receive funds are usually government or public entities or tax-exempt entities organized as 501(c)(3)s. The former include public health departments, public institutions of higher education, and public schools. The latter include tax-exempt charities or foundations themselves (one foundation giving to another foundation). If you work in a hospital or long-term care setting, you may or may not qualify for receiving a grant. Find out from your financial administrators the agency's tax status. If it is not a 501(c)(3), it may have an affiliated tax-exempt arm that can receive foundation funds. If it does not, look for a partner that is qualified as a 501(c)(3) who will serve as the fiscal agent and administrator of the grant. Tax status should not be a deterrent to seeking funds to support a good idea.

Are there additional restrictions on grant applicants?

Most foundations have geographic restrictions, and you will want to make sure that your agency resides within the region. For example, the Robert Wood Johnson Foundation funds only projects within the United States, its territories, and jurisdictions. Regional foundations fund only within their catchment area. For example, the Richmond Memorial Health Foundation funds projects in central Virginia.

Make certain that your agency is eligible to receive grant funds.

Selection criteria

"There are people who, instead of listening to what is being said to them, are already listening to what they are going to say themselves."

—Albert Guinon, playwright

As with all other components of the CFP, the selection criteria must be written specifically as the grantor requests. This is not the time to be moving forward without "listening."

The selection criteria comprise the body of proposals. If you have followed the suggestions in previous chapters, you are prepared to address each criterion. Minimally, these include a description of your agency, a needs assessment, objectives or goals and methods to achieve them, and the estimated timeline. We will examine evaluation, the budget, and other requirements in subsequent chapters.

How should you describe your agency?

Use the materials on your agency's website and in marketing materials, articles of incorporation, and other documents to describe your agency. If your agency is already a grants recipient, contact the grants office or grant recipient for a copy of the agency description from them. Don't be afraid to copy from previously written content about your organization. Tailor the description to fit your project focus. And be sure to include in this section everything that the grantor wants included.

What should you include in your needs assessment?

Use the information that you have already gathered to justify the need for your proposal. Donors like to give their money to worthy projects, so you want to make a case in the best manner possible.

We discussed this at length in Chapter 2.

What comprises the subsection on description of the project?

This section is the crux of your proposal. If you have completed the logic model template as part of your project planning process, you should be ready to write this section. Your description should be concise but inclusive of each of the components found in the logic model. Consequently, you should include the following (consult Chapter 4 for further explanation):

* The goal, intended outcome, and/or impact of the project.

* The project objectives that will need to be completed to achieve the project goal, outcome, or impact.

* Project outputs or deliverables that will be used to measure goal attainment.

* All anticipated activities that you will execute to achieve the objectives.

If you have created a logic model (See Table 4.1), you should include it in this section of your proposal to assist the grantors in visualizing your project (and also to demonstrate your carefully considered project). Some grantmakers will expect that you include the responsible parties for each objective and the timeline for each activity. Again, be sure to include everything that the grantmaker specifies in the CFP under this section.

What should you write about sustainability?

All CFPs require that you address sustainability. This should answer the question, "How will you continue this work after the funding ceases?" Grantmakers are very interested in how you plan to sustain your project post-funding. And oftentimes, we grantwriters give this section of the proposal little time and energy. Yet, one can understand why grantmakers want us to think carefully about sustaining the work. If they are going to invest in a project that has worth and is consistent with their funding priorities, why would they invest in a project where sustainability is uncertain, should it be shown that the project is a success?

If you have used a planning team in your problem identification and project planning, you are already one step ahead for sustaining your project and documenting the effort in this section. Your planning team should include partners who are willing to invest in the project, either as writers or financial contributors, or both. Stakeholders may be willing to contribute financially or with in-kind support, meaning that they will contribute individuals, resources, supplies, and so forth during grant funding and after the funding ceases. Box 5.1 contains a list of potential contributors who can assist in sustaining your work. You should be thinking about sustainability from the beginning.

5.1 Sustaining your work post-grant funding

Financial contributions

* Other foundations or nonprofit grantors

* Federal or state agencies

* Institutions such as your own

* Revenues gained from your project

* Private sector funders such as medical device or pharmaceutical companies

* In-kind contributions

* Your agency

* Other agencies involved in the project work

* Professional associations

* Volunteers

How do you describe the project staff and their qualifications?

This section of the proposal should identify who will be involved in the project. Minimally it should contain the project director and people integral to each component of the project as you envision it. Chapter 4's logic model example is a pain management improvement project that involved engaging the nursing staff in a new pain assessment tool and developing policies to implement the protocol throughout the institution. Because staff nurses are involved, we would most likely want to list a staff developer to conduct the educational component of the project, as well as someone from administration to help with the policy review and revision.

In this section, you would describe briefly the qualifications of the project staff. If you need to hire someone to fill a position, you would indicate as much and write something about the qualifications the person who fills the position needs to meet.

In this section, you want to sell the expertise and qualifications of all who will be involved on the project. Grantmakers look carefully at this section because of the investment that they will be making. They want to be assured that the appropriate individuals will be in place or hired to carry out the project.

What should be included in the plan for dissemination of outcomes?

If your project has the impact that you desire, you will want to tell others about your success. Grantmakers also want you to tell others, because they want credit for funding your project. Will you describe your project in agency newsletters or annual reports? Will you make presentations to professional associations? Will you create a website or enhance a currently existing website with your activities? Describe how you plan to tell your story, and include as many dissemination methods as you can, consistent with the project.

> **TIP** Write the selection criteria section carefully and according to the grantmaker's instructions. If possible, extract from the CFP each section's requirements and put this into your own draft, so that you have the guidelines front and center while writing each section. This is not the time for creative writing 101.

Weighting of the proposal

"If winning isn't everything, why do they keep score?"

–Vince Lombardi, football coach

How do you decide on the level of detail that should be included in each section of the proposal?

Grantwriters will usually distribute their criteria for scoring proposals. This checklist is a very useful document, because it communicates the relative importance of each section of the proposal. Table 5.1 contains a sample grantwriter's proposal assessment checklist. For this sample call for proposals, please note the following:

* The relative importance of each section.

* Seventy-five percent of the proposal will be weighted on the merits of the description of the problem; the narrative describing the project's goals, activities, and outcomes; and the evaluation plan.

* No weight is assigned to the project personnel and the budget.

Table 5.1: Proposal evaluation checklist

The XYZ Foundation Checklist for Proposal Submission

Item	Percentage	Proposal score
Description of the applicant	10	
Description of the problem needs assessment	20	
Description of the project purpose	40	
Goals and outcomes		
Objectives		
Activities		
Deliverables		
Plan for sustainability	10	
Plan for evaluation	15	
Plan for dissemination of outcomes	5	
Project personnel	0	
Budget	0	
Total	100	

It's easy to stay in our comfort zone when attacking a problem such as responding to a call for proposals. This may result in our investing more time and energy in writing about those comfort areas, such as describing our agency. This checklist tells us that while writing about the agency is important, it is only worth 10 points out of 100. *Plan to write according to the weight that is assigned to each topic area.*

In the example given, no weight is assigned to the project personnel and the budget. Do not be fooled into thinking that these two areas are not important. On the contrary, if you do not adequately address either or both of these areas, the grantmakers are likely to fail the proposal on its merits. Consequently, these two areas could be considered as important or coequal to the proposal narrative itself. The reasons for this are related to the grantmaker's assessment of the readiness and preparation of the project to be directed and carried out by the right personnel with a budget sufficiently allocated with the appropriate resources.

TIP

Keep in mind the importance reflected by the scoring weight of each section. Write your proposal accordingly.

TAKE-AWAY TIPS

✓ **Proposal writing is not a creative writing exercise.**

✓ **Make certain your purpose statement reflects the funding priorities of the grantmaker.**

✓ **While you must follow the directions in writing your proposal, your written work should "sell" your project to the grantmaker in such a way that the grantmaker is absolutely certain that you will be a good steward of the funds. Toot your horn!**

FAQs

In responding to the call for proposals, may I reorder the sections so that they flow more accurately according to my way of presenting the material?

No. Follow the directions to the letter. Do not deviate. Grantmakers review many proposals, and they become annoyed when an applicant deviates from their instructions. Remember: They give the money. You want the money. You play the game according to their rules.

What happens if I exceed the page limit in this part of the proposal?

If you exceed the page limit, one of three things is likely to happen. The best outcome would be that the grantmaker would ignore that you exceeded the page limit and permit the extension in pages. The most likely outcomes would be that either they toss out your proposal entirely, *or* they read only so far as the page limit they have set. This latter scenario would mean that they would not read all parts of the proposal and therefore would not score your proposal as high as someone whose proposal was kept within the page limits.

What should I do if I don't understand something that the grantmaker asks?

Contact the person at the foundation to ask questions. You should do this with sufficient time to gather the required information and adjust your proposal. Do not wait until the day before the proposal is due to ask a question.

What would happen if I miss a section of the proposal?

You would be graded accordingly. Not a good idea. Make certain that you address each section of the proposal.

6

*

Evaluating the Project

Do you:

Know about generic evaluation methods?

Understand how to integrate evaluation into each component of your proposed project?

Have a basic idea about how to evaluate each of the project's activities?

Appreciate the importance of following the grantmaker's request for information on how you will evaluate your project?

As part of the call for proposals (CFP), grantmakers include a section on evaluation. As I've mentioned previously, and as we learned in Chapter 1, grantmakers want reassurance that their money will be well spent. Consequently, they want you to answer this question, "How do we know that your desired outcomes and impact have been achieved?" Each proposal, therefore, contains a section on evaluation, and in the call for proposals, grantmakers will tell you how much weight they attach to evaluation. All puns aside, the weight for evaluation is usually hefty, so this section is one that you will want to think through and write very carefully. In this chapter, we briefly describe a generic form of evaluation using logic model terminology (see Chapter 4), another common evaluation model (the CIPP model), and grantmakers' evaluation requirements.

Glossary

Context evaluation: Collection of data to determine the worth of a project or the need for the project.

Evaluation: Systematic method for collecting, analyzing, and using information to answer questions about a project.

Input evaluation: Assessment of the components of a project that are integral to the foundation of the project, such as the assumptions and external environment. Used interchangeably with context evaluation.

Process evaluation: Assessment of activities designed to achieve project objectives.

Product evaluation: Assessment of data collected to determine the effectiveness of the project in meeting its outcomes or achieving intended impact.

Summative evaluation: See product evaluation.

Evaluation models

"One of the great mistakes is to judge policies and programs by their intentions rather than their results."

—Milton Friedman, economist and Nobel laureate

What comprises the generic evaluation paradigm?

Depending upon the discipline, evaluation takes many forms. However, in its essence, evaluation consists of three systems model elements: outputs, users, and results (Rennie & Singh, 1995). Figure 6.1 demonstrates the relationship among the three; it also highlights that different models employ different terminology. The glossary highlights the terminology equivalents that are used in differing evaluation models. In this generic evaluation model, the evaluation consists of determining whether or not the user received the outputs and whether or not the user used the outputs to achieve results.

Outputs (deliverables) ⟶ **Users** (subjects) ⟶ **Results** (impact)

Figure 6.1   Evaluation process

Evaluation itself is a process, and it is most effective when you conceptualize it as a parallel and dynamic progression within the project itself. You conceive of your project as one in which the goal or potential impact is foremost in your thinking. Consequently, each activity has an evaluative component, answering the question "Is it working?" At the completion of each part (objective or outcome) of the project, you ask whether that particular outcome was achieved or whether it worked.

What comprises the CIPP evaluation model?

The CIPP model (Stufflebeam, 2007) is a simple systems model that further explains the generic evaluation model template. A basic open system includes input (including the context), process, and output. The acronym, CIPP, originates in the terms; context (C), input (I), process (P), and product (P).

In writing your proposal, you have already conducted the first two components of the CIPP evaluation model. Context evaluation is the type of evaluation that you conduct as you make the case to the funder for the worthiness of your project. It includes examining and describing the context of the project you are evaluating, conducting a needs assessment, determining the goals and objectives of the project, and ascertaining whether the proposed objectives will be sufficiently responsive to the identified needs. Input evaluation includes such activities as your description of the resources you have and will need and the mission of the organization and its congruence with your project. Context evaluation answers the questions "Is this a worthy project?" and "Have we determined what we need to execute the project?"

Process evaluation includes activities designed to calculate how the project is progressing once you begin implementation. It might include such items as course evaluation, patient vital signs after treatments, and interviews with the project participants during selected portions of the project. Input evaluation provides information about what is actually occurring in the project. Based on the results of measures throughout the project, you may decide to make changes that you believe will improve the final outcomes. In general, process evaluation helps in making implementation

TIP: You want to make sure that every activity you undertake in your project has an evaluative component. Measure the effectiveness of the activity and make changes as needed to increase its effectiveness next time.

decisions or data-based decisions about project activities. In some evaluation circles, process evaluation is known as formative evaluation. Process evaluation answers the question "Is it working?"

Product evaluation includes determining and examining the general and specific outcomes of the project. Product evaluation seeks to determine whether the project itself made the impact or achieved the results that you intended to accomplish when you designed the project. It involves measuring anticipated outcomes, attempting to identify unanticipated outcomes, and assessing the merits of the project. Product evaluation is very helpful in making summative evaluation decisions. It answers the questions "Did it work?" and "Should the project be continued?" Additional Internet sources on evaluation models are listed in Box 6.1.

(6.1) Additional sources on evaluation models

* Evaluation designs. Hansen (2005) describes a series of evaluation models that can be adapted for different types of projects. The abstract and access to the full article are available at
http://evi.sagepub.com/content/11/4/447.short.
The full article costs $25, but it may be worth the expenditure if you want to examine various models.

* Evaluation models checklists from the Evaluation Center at Western Michigan University, available at
http://www.wmich.edu/evalctr/checklists/evaluation-models/.
This site has links to the CIPP model and other evaluation types. Since the CIPP model is commonly used, the checklist may be very useful if your grantmaker requires the use of this model.

Integrating evaluation into your proposal

"The most serious mistakes are not being made as a result of wrong answers. The truly dangerous thing is asking the wrong question"

–Peter Drucker, management consultant

How do you put it all together?

Using the logic model example illustrated in Chapter 4 and depicted in Box 4.1, you can see that evaluation is ongoing and continual. For each activity in your project in which you have described selected outputs, determine how you will conduct a process or formative evaluation. For each expected result (outcome), discuss how you will measure whether and how the project will be successful. Box 6.2 contains a matrix that depicts integration of process evaluation activities as they contribute to the overall summative evaluation of the outcomes and impact in the pain management example from Chapter 4.

> **TIP** Think of evaluation as a series of data collection points that help guide the project in its intended direction. Do not forget to assess the data; collecting data is one thing, but analyzing the information and making changes are the real reasons we evaluate our work.

6.2 Evaluation matrix

Pain management improvement is a project designed to engage the nursing staff in implementing a pain assessment protocol that improves the identification and management of pain in all patients in our agency. Our project is a strategic initiative that requires a strategic evaluation. As shown in the following matrix, there are six strategic evaluation questions to be answered by the project. We will craft the detailed evaluation design, develop survey and interview tools, manage data collection and analysis, and produce evaluation reports.

Evaluation Questions and Data Sources

Evaluation question	Patient pain management data	Research literature on pain assessment and management practices	Patient satisfaction surveys at 6, 12, and 18 months	Documentation of inputs, activities, outputs, and outcomes	Strategic review of evaluation results by project steering committee
Do the stakeholders see value in implementing a plan that ultimately reduces patient pain by effective pain assessment and management?	✓	✓	✓	✓	✓
Has the agency selected a revised pain assessment and management protocol that is based on evidence?		✓	✓	✓	✓
Have the educational programs changed nurses' pain assessment and management practices?		✓		✓	✓
Are policy changes in place that support improved pain assessment and management protocols?				✓	✓
Do patients describe their pain management experience in the agency improved over pre-project levels?	✓		✓	✓	✓
Have the lessons learned been disseminated broadly?				✓	✓

Funder requirements

"There is no shame in taking orders from those who themselves have learned to obey."

—William Edward Forster, industrialist and philanthropist

What do grantmakers usually ask for in the evaluation section of the CFP?

In reading through this portion of the call for proposals, look for the following:

* Does the grantmaker require that a percentage of your grant funding be allocated to evaluation?

* Is there a requirement for an external evaluator whom you will need to hire?

* Will you be required to follow a certain evaluation model?

* What sorts of key words does the grantmaker use in the call-for-proposal terminology related to evaluation? Examples include "deliverables," "outputs," "timeline," and "responsible persons." Have you fully addressed each of the descriptors in the funder's call for proposals as it relates to evaluation?

References

Hansen, H. F. (2005). Choosing evaluation models: A discussion on evaluation design. *Evaluation, 11*(4), 447–462.

Rennie, J. K., & Singh, N. C. (1995). Empowering communities for sustainable livelihoods. In *Community adaptation and sustainable livelihoods.* Retrieved from http://www.iisd.org/casl/caslguide/evalmodel.htm

Stufflebeam, D. (2007). *CIPP evaluation model checklist.* Retrieved from http://www.wmich.edu/evalctr/archive_checklists/cippchecklist_mar0%pdf

TAKE-AWAY TIPS

✓ **Grantmakers take evaluation seriously. The reasons for their awarding funds for notable projects usually lie in how well they believe that the grantees will be able to achieve their outcomes. And how well they achieve these outcomes is based on the measures they use to monitor success; hence, the evaluation plan.**

✓ **Understand the essential terms focused on evaluation, especially those that are synonyms. Don't become frustrated by the interchangeable use of the terms. Decide on which terms you will use in your proposal and stick with them.**

✓ **Think of evaluation like working a jigsaw puzzle. All the pieces have to fit together to make a complete picture. If you try to put two pieces together that don't work, you know you've made an error (formative or process evaluation). When you've completed the entire puzzle, you've successfully completed summative or product evaluation. Make sure you follow the grantmaker's evaluation requirements to the letter. There are no shortcuts on evaluation.**

FAQs

Do grantmakers ask that I follow a specific evaluation model? What if I have no experience with that particular model?

Sometimes grantmakers will ask for a specific model. If you have no experience with that model, you should (1) read up on it; (2) see if you can enlist someone to help who has experience with the model; and (3) contact the grantmaker's project officer to ask for clarification and suggestions for learning more about the model.

Do I have to be an evaluation expert to submit a proposal?

No. If you have no experience in evaluation techniques consistent with the activities that you will be performing, find someone who has that expertise and write them into the proposal as a contract evaluation consultant. Ask that expert for assistance in developing the evaluation content so that it will be aligned with his or her responsibilities if the grant is awarded. An evaluation expert will also be able to provide assistance in developing a viable evaluation model for your particular project. Seek funding from a partner to assist in this if you can.

7

✳

The Budget

Do you:

Understand terms associated with budgets?

Know how to develop and analyze a budget?

Understand the difference between "match" and "in-kind"?

Know how to convert your project personnel and activities into a specific dollar amount?

Know how to develop a line-item budget and write a supporting budget narrative?

A primary reason that you seek grants to help resolve practice or education pet peeves, further nursing science, or whatever your motivation for your project is to obtain external funds to support the project. Consequently, the budget in your proposal is a critical component of the document. This chapter outlines the major components of the budget and provides tips for creating a budget that will pass muster with the grantmaker and provide you with the funds you need to carry out your work.

Glossary

Computer hardware and office equipment: Some funders require that these outlays are itemized and explained fully, so that their purchase can be deemed essential to the operation of the project. When it comes to purchasing technology tools, some funders may require a description of the time the computer will be used specifically for the project. Funders can require that the budget amount requested represent the percentage of time for which the technology will be used for the project.

Consultant/contract expenses: These expenses are usually calculated at a flat or hourly rate and are contracted out of the agency without any fringe benefits.

Direct costs: Costs that can be assigned to a specific cost center. In grantmaking, direct costs usually refer to personnel and fringe benefits.

Income: Funds that accrue to the agency as a result of project activity, such as tuition charges.

Indirect costs: A portion of the funder's grant allocation that is used to operate the project for such items as office space and overhead. Some funders do not permit any grant funds to be used for indirect costs. Others cap the costs at a certain percent or amount.

In-kind (or contributed) costs: These are contributions from your agency and other partners. Some funders require a certain match, such as 1:1, meaning that you seek $1 in funding for every $1 that is donated to the project.

In-kind costs are typically "donated" from agencies, such as paying for a person's time allocated to the project, or other donations, such as meeting space, refreshments, and so forth. Other costs are contributed, such as real cash.

Nonpersonnel direct costs: The amount of grant funding allocated toward the direct operation of the funded project, such as meeting and travel expenses, printing and copying, and computer software.

Personnel: The amount of funding allocated toward compensating project personnel who are part of the funded agency. Personnel costs are generally calculated based on the person's time devoted to the project as a percent of that person's salary, plus a prorated portion of his or her fringe benefits.

Budget overview

"A budget tells us what we can't afford, but it doesn't keep us from buying it."

–William Feather, author and publisher

How important is the budget in the overall project proposal?

The budget is a critical and coequal partner to the proposal narrative, and it is designed to direct us to stay within our spending limits. Some reviewers read the budget first, before reading the entire proposal, so you want to make sure that the budget can stand on its own. If your project description meets the grantmaker's requirements, the budget should reflect an allocation of funds commensurate with the activities that you will be undertaking.

You will divide your budget section into two parts: a line-item budget (see Table 7.1 for an example) and the budget narrative. The former is a visual display of how the grant and contributed funds will support the project. The latter is a written account that further describes the figures cited in the line-item budget.

Unless you work with budgets on a regular basis, you may not be familiar with budget terms. Consult the glossary for explanations of budget terms.

Table 7.1   Sample line-item budget

Line items	Grant amount	Match support	Total
PERSONNEL			
Project Director (0.1 FTE)	5,000	5,000	10,000
Project Coordinator/Staff Developer (0.25 FTE)	10,000	5,000	15,000
Administrative staff (0.15 FTE)		5,000	5,000
Fringe benefits (calculated at 35%)	5,250	5,250	10,500
Subtotal direct costs	20,250	20,250	40,500
OTHER DIRECT COSTS			
Office operations		5,000	5,000
Project space		5,000	5,000
Communications and marketing		1,000	1,000
Printing		500	500
Equipment		2,000	2,000
Meeting/classroom expenses		5,000	5,000
Travel			
Airfare	2,000		2,000
Hotel and per diem	1,000		1,000
Subtotal indirect costs	3,000	18,500	21,500

Line items	Grant amount	Match support	Total
PURCHASED (CONTRACTED) SERVICES			
Pain management consultant (4 days @ $500/day)	1,000	1,000	2,000
Materials and supplies for workshop (folders & contents) 50 @ $2.00		100	100
Subtotal contract services	1,000	1,100	2,100
Subtotal direct costs	24,250	39,850	64,100
Indirect costs	750		750
Total Costs	25,000	39,850	64,850

How important is the "match" or "contributions" of funds and resources from other sources?

In addition to asking for a specific amount of grant funds, grantmakers usually require some sort of match, either as a monetary match or as in-kind support. Grantmakers consider these requirements as a means of determining how resolute the applicants are in support of the project. That is, how much skin are the applicants willing to put in the game to assure the success of the project? Match requirements may be stringent, such as a 1:1 ($1 of grant funds for every $1 of applicant funds) match, or more lenient (any ratio less than 1:1).

Some grantmakers consider in-kind support as part of the match. Robust in-kind support also denotes stakeholder commitment. Your agency and your stakeholders may provide any sort of in-kind support, such as physical space for offices or labs, meeting space, refreshments for meetings, their own travel to meetings, and other technical support, such as IT expertise. Make sure you delineate each item of match support and place a monetary value on

TIP Consider the budget as a separate and coequal document to your proposal narrative. Keep both documents congruent and complementary to one another.

it. Some grantmakers will ask that you categorize support as in-kind and match; others simply seek a total contribution from the applicants.

Budget specifics

"Money is a terrible master but an excellent servant."

—P. T. Barnum, showman and circus owner

When creating the budget, weigh the grantmakers' stated awards (in cash) against the work required in your proposed project and the amount of match and in-kind support your agency and partners are willing to invest. Grantmakers usually require both for all parts of the budget—the request from the grantmaker and the match. For each projected cost, you will cite the total amount that will be invested and how much will be sought from the grantmaker and how you will contribute. You will display these figures in the line-item budget and describe them in more detail in the budget narrative.

What comprises direct and indirect costs?

In addition to requiring a match, grantmakers usually divide budgets minimally into two categories: direct and indirect costs. Direct costs are those that are associated with cost centers and include such items as personnel, travel and meeting costs, office supplies, and telephone.

Grantmakers may or may not permit expensing indirect costs, which are charges to the project not associated with any specific line item. Sometimes these are perceived as the cost of doing business, administrative costs, or overhead costs (to cover such items as utilities). If a grantmaker permits indirect costs to be expensed to the project, be sure to allocate only the percent allowed and no more. Check with your agency administrators; they may waive the indirect costs, in which case you will be able to invest all of the funds directly into supporting your project.

Some grantmakers assign other categories for budgets. These might include contract costs (for hiring consultants to assist in the project work), capital costs (for bricks and mortar), and equipment costs (for purchasing equipment, such as microscopes, projectors, laptop computers, and smartboards). Do not charge an item to a grant that the grantmaker prohibits, such as bricks and mortar to build a simulation laboratory.

How should you account for personnel?

For most projects, except those that will consist of the purchase of expensive equipment, personnel comprise a significant expense to the project. However, you will not execute the project without personnel possessing the right expertise and the right amount of time devoted to the project. Here are the steps you should take:

* Consider who must be involved and whether you will expense all or part of their time to the project.

* Calculate how much time they will need to invest (consult your logic model or project activities to determine their level of involvement).

* Based on their current salary, calculate the total amount of their salary devoted to the project and then separate that figure into how much of the funds you will seek from the grantmaker and how much the employer will be willing to contribute as a match.

* Calculate the fringe benefits similarly. From your human resources department, you will find out the fringe benefits percentage package contributed by the employer (fringes include health insurance, group life, and employer FICA contribution) and use that percent of the total salary to determine how much you will seek from the grantmaker and how much will be donated by the employer.

Once you have calculated the personnel costs and inserted them into the line-item budget, describe the personnel contributions in the budget narrative. Plan to write a brief paragraph for each person identified in the personnel costs. For example, in our pain management example, we might say the following about the project director:

> The project director for this work will be Ms. Jones, the pain management clinical nurse specialist for our agency. She will be responsible for the overall execution of the project. In addition to assuring that project objectives and activities are implemented, she will be responsible for developing and executing the project evaluation plan and writing the policies and procedures for the use of the assessment tool in our agency. Ms. Jones will devote 10% of her time to the project: 5% to the grant, and 5% as an in-kind contribution.

By writing the description of the project director in this manner, you will have delineated specific project activities to Ms. Jones, as well as allocated funds consistent with her responsibilities. Thus, the grant reviewer should be able to visualize the link between the logic model in Chapter 4, the narrative in your proposal (Chapter 5), the evaluation activities (Chapter 6), and finally the allocation of funds for the work in the budget.

What will you include in other direct costs?

The answer to this question, of course, is *it depends*. Follow these steps to determine what you will seek from the grantmaker, your employer, and your partners:

* Review your logic model to determine the specific activities that you will undertake in the project. Will you need to travel? Will you hold meetings? Will you develop marketing materials? Will you create printed or copied products? Will project participants need electronic devices (that are not already available)?

* Once you have determined what these specific items will be, figure out how much it will cost to accomplish each one. You may need to gather additional information here, depending upon what the specific items are. For example, if you propose to purchase notebook computers, consult several retail hardware websites to estimate the range of costs for notebook computers, and select a midrange price. Use the same methodology for other expenses.

* Then determine how much you should (or can) charge to the grant and how much will be contributed or offered as a cash match from partner agencies.

* Put that all together on your line-item budget and write a brief description that explains each cost in your budget narrative.

How do you determine the estimated costs of specific items that are direct costs?

You will want to estimate these costs as accurately as possible, although they will be estimates at best. However, you should resist the temptation of pulling costs out of the air. Here are some hints:

> **Travel costs.** You should be able to determine how many miles individuals will need to travel and who will be eligible for travel reimbursement. Use the agency travel reimbursement figures per mile for automobile travel. For travel by airplane, find out the average cost of travel for eligible project participants and use those figures. In your budget narrative, indicate how you arrived at the travel costs by stating what sources you used and how many people you will reimburse for how many miles. Leave nothing to chance.

> **Meeting costs.** Find out the rental costs for the spaces you will use, the charges for renting audiovisual equipment, and the charges for food. If a partnering agency will be contributing these

items, ask them to estimate the amount that they will contribute and use that in your line-item budget. State the source of your estimate in your budget narrative.

Office operations. This might include such items as use of the copy machine, telephone charges, and purchase of software to operate the computers. For copying, use either a prorated cost of renting the copier or a cost per page for each copy based on an estimated number of copies that you will generate. Use the same methodology for telephone expenses: Determine the monthly charge for long-distance and how many phones you will use, and estimate how many calls you will make. Again, justify the costs for each in your budget narrative.

Computer equipment purchases. State how many pieces of equipment you will purchase, how they will be used to support the project activities, and the estimated cost of each. When estimating the costs, use a reasonable figure from your agency supply department or from another vendor.

By now you have most likely determined that there is a method to estimating costs. The values inherent in the method include honesty and transparency. Be honest in your estimated costs of each activity and err on the side of providing too much information to the grantmaker (transparency).

How do you determine indirect costs?

Indirect costs are usually simple to calculate. Consult with the grantmaker's requirements for indirect costs and use that figure. If a grantmaker indicates that no more than 5% of the direct costs can be allocated to indirect costs, calculate the total direct costs and add 5% as indirect costs.

Watch out for the catch. Sometimes grantmakers will indicate that no more than a certain percent may be allocated to indirect costs, and the total amount for the grant award cannot exceed a certain amount of money. In our line-item budget example in Box 7.1, the total amount allocated to indirect costs is $750. In this hypothetical situation, the grantmaker has indicated that the maximum grant to be awarded is $25,000 and that 5% may be allocated to indirect costs. However, in the example, the total sum prior to calculating the indirect costs is $24,250. Hence, the applicant is seeking only $750 in indirect costs.

Just how much the applicant's agency will seek in indirect costs may determine how much the applicant may seek in direct costs. In the example we have just described, the agency might indicate that it requires the full 5% in indirect costs. In that case, the applicant would have to adjust the other direct costs downward to accommodate the agency's requirement.

In summary, establishing the budget for the project is a process that consists of analyzing the project's activities, assigning a dollar value to them, and then determining how to allocate the funds. Follow the grantmaker's instructions on the match and in-kind contributions. Finally, make certain that you ask for funds to support activities permitted for funding.

TIP

Think of your budget as a means of quantifying the resources that will be used to execute your project. Use the line-item budget as a skeletal representation of the resources and the budget narrative as the flesh on the skeleton's bones.

TAKE-AWAY TIPS

✓ **Do not use your budget to acquire resources that cannot be traced directly to the project itself. For example, do not seek funding for a projector for a project that has no presentations or training programs associated with it.**

✓ **Do not assign a project director to the position and allocate a small percentage to that person's time unless you can justify the small percentage of time with other personnel offsets. For example, do not seek 5% funding for the project director and list 10 responsibilities for that person.**

✓ **Do not seek funds for capital construction of a simulation laboratory if the funder specifically states that no funds can be used for construction.**

✓ **Do not seek funds for travel that includes more trips than are listed on the project activities.**

✓ **Do not seek funds for indirect costs that exceed the funder's stated indirect cost allocation.**

FAQs

Can the budget narrative and project narrative ever look like two separate documents, not in synch with one another?

That would make for a very poor proposal submission. When you write your proposal narrative that contains the activities you intend to undergo, you should be thinking about what resources (human, technical, organizational, and so forth) are needed to complete each activity. Each will require an investment of money, either directly or indirectly. These should be quantified in the budget narrative.

If the grantmaker does not require a match of any kind, should we quantify one anyway?

Yes. Occasionally grantmakers are willing to fund an entire project without any donation from the applicant or its partners. That is an ideal, but rare, situation. You should write the types of donations in time, cash, and people to the project even if the grantmaker does not ask for it. Doing so will help you project and account for the contributions of yourself and your partners while the project is ongoing. It will also help in the long run, as you plan for sustaining your work post-funding.

If we need something for our project that the grantmaker indicates it does not fund, such as capital costs, may we ask for the funds anyway?

You may, but you will not get them. And you may irritate the grantmaker, who may think that you have not read the requirements. If you need something that the grantmaker does not fund, seek funding from another source, such as a partner.

What should we do if we cannot obtain an accurate estimate for some expense that we want to charge to the grant?

Do the best you can, describe in your budget narrative what you did to obtain an estimate, and indicate the degree of certainty for the estimate you are giving.

Will it be possible to move budget items around from line to line after we get funded and need to make adjustments?

In the event that your project is awarded funds, the grantmaker will meet with you to discuss how to administer your grant and whether changes will be permitted to your budget, under what circumstances, and how much can be changed in budget items. This is usually a negotiable process.

8

✳

Putting On the Final Touches

Do you:

Know the grantmaker's submission requirements?

Know which method of proposal submission you should execute?

Understand which items must be placed in the proposal appendices?

Have a plan for proposal quality assurance prior to submitting the proposal?

In this chapter, we tie together the loose ends of the proposal submission. Congratulate yourself on arriving at this point; if you have been working on your proposal in a linear manner according to the chapters in this book, you are at the endpoint prior to submission. However, if you have been reading your grantmaker's requirements for proposal submission, you have been collecting the information required in the proposal, so you should be ready to put the final pieces of the proposal puzzle together. This chapter reviews the grantmaker's submission requirements and supporting materials.

Glossary

Biographical information: Information on project personnel named in the budget. Funders may provide a form to use for this information.

Budget narrative: Description of how funds will be expended to meet project objectives. The narrative should complement and be consistent with the proposal narrative.

Line-item budget: The project budget laid out in spreadsheet format. The funder may require use of specific forms or subsections. Include both requested funds and funds that will be in-kind or match to meet the funder's requirements.

Proposal narrative: The main body of the proposal that describes each required section of the proposal.

Support letters: Communication from each project partner, outlining the role played in proposal development and the role to be played, should funding be awarded.

Transmittal letter: Introductory letter from either the project director or the chief administrative officer of the agency.

Submission requirements

*"I am one of those people who thrive on
deadlines; nothing brings on inspiration more
readily than desperation."*

—Harry Shearer, actor

What are the typical proposal submission requirements?

Submission requirements refer to the grantmaker's guidelines for
the structure and appearance of your proposal. These requirements
differ for each grantmaker but follow a general pattern. Follow the
requirements closely. Submitting a proposal using your own system
is not creativity; it is ignorance and can result in the elimination of
your proposal. In the next few paragraphs, we will discuss each
requirement.

> *Structural requirements:* These include page
> length, fonts, margins, spacing, margin
> justification, and in some cases, word or character
> counts. Follow the guidelines explicitly. The only
> exception to strict structural requirements is the
> appendices. These do not have to adhere to the
> narrative requirements, unless there is a total page
> length for appendices.

> *Use of grantmaker forms:* Some grantmakers
> require that you use their forms for some or all
> parts of the proposal. If so, use the forms, unless
> the grantmaker permits otherwise.

> *Number of copies:* Check carefully the
> requirement for the number of copies. This
> requirement does not apply if you are sending
> your proposal electronically. Otherwise, make
> sure that you submit the required number of
> copies, in addition to the signed original.

Transmittal or cover letter: Most grantmakers require that this letter be included in the proposal submission. Usually the letter is signed by the chief executive officer of the applicant agency or designee. The letter itself is simple in format. Consult Box 8.1 for a sample letter.

(8.1) *Sample transmittal or cover letter*

XYZ Foundation

December 12, 2011

Ms. Jane Smith, Program Officer
The XYZ Foundation
123 Grant Avenue
Foundationsburg, ME 12345

Dear Ms. Smith:

On behalf of the Applicant Agency, I am pleased to send this proposal to the XYZ Foundation as a response to your call for proposals for innovative ways to manage pain among patients with chronic conditions. We are requesting $25,000 from the XYZ Foundation. With a match of $39,850 from our agency and our partners, we believe that we will have the resources to carry out our project consistent with your foundation's mission and program goals.

Enclosed are our proposal, budget, and supporting documentation. This proposal has the full support of our administration and my office.

Please do not hesitate to contact me if you have questions.

Sincerely yours,

Gloria Jones

Gloria Jones, DNP, RN
Applicant Agency Director of Nursing Research

How do you make sure the proposal arrives at the grant-maker on time?

Submission date: You may always submit *prior* to the submission date, but do not miss the deadline or your proposal will not be considered. Make sure you understand what time zone that the grantmaker is using. Close-of-business for applicants submitting on the West Coast of the United States to the East Coast entails the loss of 3 hours, so factor that into your submission equation.

Electronic submission: Increasingly, grantmakers are permitting or requiring electronic submission. Depending upon the method and software used, you may have to navigate uncertain waters, such as obtaining a user identification and password prior to submission and utilizing an electronic format for some or all of the proposal components. Make certain that you give yourself adequate time to upload each section of the required materials. Since applicants routinely wait until the last minute to submit their proposals, the grantmaker's system may be overloaded; do not wait until the last minute to hit the send button.

Submission by mail: Submission of proposals by mail is fraught with its own uncertainties as well, so you will want to make sure that you account for any unintended eventuality. Use priority or express mail instead of regular mail; it's well worth the expense, and you will have a means of tracking electronically or via a written receipt. Again, make sure you give yourself at least one extra day, just in case.

TIP Make sure you have completed all the submission requirements according to the grantmaker's instructions.

In-person submission: You can always hand deliver your proposal, although this method is not without its own set of anxieties. Make sure that the person receiving the proposal knows where it goes and gives you a receipt.

Supporting materials

"There are thousands of grant programs, and every program has different requirements and deadlines."

—Matthew Lesko, entertainer

In addition to your proposal narrative and budget, you will need to send other types of materials that are either required or designed to enhance your proposal's attractiveness to the grantmaker. Typically these materials comprise the appendices. Make sure that you do not exceed the page length for appendices, if there is one.

What is usually required for supporting materials?

Essential documents verifying applicant eligibility status for receiving grants: As a condition of their own tax-exempt status, the federal government requires that grantmakers issue grants only to agencies that fall within certain tax-exempt status. We discussed tax exemption in Chapter 5, and the documentation for the tax status will be part of the supporting materials. Usually the grantmaker will require a copy of the federal tax-exempt status, or if your agency is a public entity such as a public university, you will need to send a copy of the organizing document. Depending upon what your agency's tax-exempt status is, you may be required to send a copy of your most recent audited financial statement.

Identification of personnel associated with the project: You will most likely be required to submit a list of your agency's board of directors and its officers, including their names, credentials, and contact information.

Biographical information on the project personnel: The nature of the information varies; some grantmakers require a sketch or copies of résumés, while others require that you complete biographical data on forms they provide. You want to assure the grantmaker that you have qualified personnel with education and experience to carry out the project activities. If you write a sketch for each person on the project, be sure to include the following:

* Name and academic credentials

* Position in the agency

* Qualifications of the individual as they relate to the role of the person in the project

* Previous grant management and implementation experience

A note on project personnel: If you do not have a person named for one of the project positions, explain that the role will be filled once you obtain funding. Then describe the qualifications that you will be seeking in the person.

Identification of partners: You want to make sure that the grantmaker knows that you have partners to help in carrying out your project. These may be individuals who are members of your project planning team, representatives from external agencies with an interest in your project,

and/or individuals representing agencies that
pledge support (either match or in-kind) for your
project. List each of your partners and include
their credentials, title, and agency.

You can strengthen your proposal and enhance your attractiveness
to the grantmaker by including letters of support from your partners. Obtaining well-written letters of support is an art form in and
of itself. Ideally these letters should communicate the following:

* A description of the partnering agency

* The role that the person has played to date in the development
  of the project (if the person has played a role)

* The importance and relevance of the project to the agency

* How the agency will assist in implementing the project, once
  the project is funded

In an effort to receive letters of support, you should resist the
temptation to write a sample letter and have the partner "fill in the
blanks" for the four bullet items mentioned above. Unfortunately,
what sometimes happens when you write a sample is that you get
just that: the sample, verbatim, with the blanks filled in. To the proposal reviewer, these letters look like they were extracted solely from
the template without much thought given to them. They will not enhance your proposal's attractiveness. At the same time, you do want
to communicate clearly about what the letter of support needs to
state to make your case for a grant award. You can have a coaching
conversation with supporting agencies, sharing information about
your project that will enable them to write a strong letter of support.

Is there additional information that you want to include in your appendices?

Some applicants include other information that they believe will
be helpful in explaining their project but are unable to "fit" into
the proposal requirements. For example, you might have the

results of a survey that help inform the need for the project. The survey results could go into an appendix. Or you might want to include a table with more information about your project, such as responsible persons for each activity and a timeline of when you plan to conduct each activity. You may also include articles assembled during the literature review that reflect information significant to your project. So long as you do not exceed page limits, incorporate any documents that enhance your project.

TIP

Supporting materials are just that; they support or undergird the merits of your proposal. Be sure to include them.

Perform one last check before clicking the "send" button

"*This does make me very very careful, particularly in the second draft, to get it right, because you do feel that somebody in the future who may be extremely important for everybody is going to have me behind them, and this is a responsibility, a huge one.*"

—Diana Wynne Jones, Writer

Are there additional words of wisdom before you send your proposal to the grantmaker?

Regardless of how you submit your proposal, spend a few extra minutes carefully reviewing each section, comparing it with the grantmaker's requirements. Have someone else conduct this exercise as well. This may sound paranoid, but there is nothing worse than spending weeks or months developing a project proposal to solve your practice or education pet peeve and sending it off, only to find that a section was omitted.

Some grantmakers include a checklist for your convenience to remind you about each required proposal section. If you have one, use it.

TIP

You may relax after you send the proposal. Until then, prepare and be ready for anything to happen.

Keep a hard and electronic copy of your proposal for your own records. If a funder has questions, you will want your proposal in front of you when you answer them. If you continue to pursue grant funding, content you have previously developed can serve as a resource or be repurposed for the next proposal.

Best wishes on a successful proposal submission!

TAKE-AWAY TIPS

✓ **Do not wait until 10 minutes before the proposal is due to submit it. Aim for 5 days in advance. That way, Murphy's Law, which is bound to happen, will run its course before you submit.**

✓ **Make absolutely certain that you follow the grantmaker's instructions for number of pages, font size, spacing, margin size, and justification. Do not stray.**

✓ **Be sure to include everything that the grantmaker requires in your proposal. If there is no proposal checklist, compose one yourself and follow it. Have someone double-check your proposal sections, including the appendices.**

✓ **Make sure you have letters of support from the major project personnel and partners. Give them a deadline for getting their letters to you well enough in advance of the deadline, so that you can check one more thing off your list prior to submission. Be a pest for those who delay.**

FAQs

I heard that there is an informal rule that one cannot start working on a proposal until 2 weeks before it's due. Is this true?

No, although people who write proposals usually have busy lives with their day jobs, and sometimes they put off until tomorrow what they should be doing today. The optimal scenario is one in which you have a list of problems that you would like to solve, a group of people you can count on to help you flesh out the specifics, and an eye for what types of funding are available. Then, when an opportunity arises, you have an infrastructure in place to start working on the proposal immediately. Waiting until 2 weeks before the proposal is due is stressful and will not promote healthy living habits.

Is there ever a grace period or permission for people to submit proposals after the deadline?

No.

What would happen to my proposal if I forget a section and realize the mistake *after* the deadline has expired?

You are probably out of luck. However, you can try contacting the program officer, whom you should know, if you have been following the suggestions in this book, and ask if there is any way that you can send, e-mail, or fax the missing section. Hope springs eternal. Otherwise, you can hope for the next grant cycle. Or find another grantmaker.

What would happen if I do not receive some letters of support from partners?

Continue to ask for them; do not let them off the hook. Submit your proposal without these letters and make a note in the appendix that other letters are forthcoming. If you are selected to receive a site visit or if the grantmakers are interested in your project, they may ask at a later time for the letters. You can deliver them to the grantmakers at that time. That said, do your best to get those letters. Not including them may reflect negatively on your proposal score.

9

✳

Excelling at a Site Visit

Do you:

Know what comprises a site visit?

Know what to do in preparation for a site visit?

Know how to demonstrate your project's worth during a site visit?

You have received word from a grantmaker that your agency will receive a site visit. This is good news, because it means that your proposal is among the semifinalists for funding—that the proposal has met minimal requirements, and it is now time to separate the wheat from the chaff among the proposals. This chapter will describe the types of site visits, what you can expect, and how you can improve your chances of being funded.

Glossary

> **Reverse site visit:** Field trip the proposal writing team takes to a central location to meet with grantmakers to validate the contents of a proposal and seek additional clarifying information.
>
> **Site visit:** Field trip grantmakers take to potential grantees for the same purpose as a reverse site visit. The "trip" can be taken also via conference call.

Preparation for a site visit

What are site visits, and what forms do they take?

"A thousand words will not leave so deep an impression as one deed."

–Henrik Ibsen

Representatives of the grantmaker conduct site visits with the proposal writing team. Depending upon the type of proposal, these visits may be made in person at the agency and may last for a workday or more, but usually do not exceed 1½ days. Alternatively, site visits may be conducted through conference calls lasting no more than several hours. Conference call "visits" are conducted with people who already know one another, perhaps by grantees who are seeking additional funds for a new project.

In reverse site visits, the proposal team meets with grantmaker representatives, usually in a neutral setting at a central location. Regardless of the format, site visits are used to confirm what is written in the proposal and ask additional questions that arise from reading the proposal. Only serious contenders receive site visits, so make sure that you shine the best light on your proposed project.

How should you prepare for a site visit?

"A winning effort begins with preparation."
—Joe Gibbs

Malcolm Gladwell, in his book *Blink* (2005), writes about the kind of rapid thinking that occurs in the blink of an eye, or the impression that you get when you meet someone for the first time or enter a room. He writes about the weird power of first impressions. A site visit can serve the same purpose. Although it lasts a bit longer than 2 seconds, the site visit is a way to show off your proposed project and all its component parts—the idea, the need, the partners, the agency, and the difference the project will make in the lives of the people it affects. You want the grantmaker visitors to be totally impressed with your project.

> **TIP** No matter what form they take, site visits are golden opportunities to highlight your proposal. Make sure you are well prepared.

When you receive notice that you will have a site visit, obtain clarity on the following:

* **Format:** In person, via conference call, or reverse site visit.

* **Length:** How long will the visit be?

* **Attendees:** Who will be attending from the grantmaker? Which proposal partners should attend?

* **Agenda:** The grantmakers are likely to suggest the agenda. If they do not, present an agenda to them that consists of a review of the proposal components, a visit to the agency (except for conference call or reverse site visit), and time for questions.

* **Miscellaneous:** Will you offer food? Will the visitors need help selecting lodging and transportation? (You will not have to pay for these expenses.) Will they require additional information before the meeting, such as financials or names and titles of persons from the team and agency?

TIP Like good scouts, you want to be prepared for a site visit. Your goals are to put life into your proposal—to give it a face for the visitors—and to create a good impression.

The most important job for you prior to the visit is to make certain that critical project partners will be available for the visit and that everyone involved knows the part he or she will play. Assign each section of the proposal to the appropriate team member, and require each person to have a speaking role in the meeting. Anticipate questions for each part of the proposal with the team, and work out the answers in advance. Practice presentations whenever possible.

Who are the site visitors, and what should you know about them?

You will know in advance who your visitors are. Use the time to find out about them. Typically, they will be program officers, members of the grantmaker's governing board, and members of an advisory committee to the grantmaker or for the project. Ask these questions: What are their backgrounds? Are any of them experts in your particular area of concern? What have they published? You can use the information to help tailor your remarks, based on what you have learned about them.

The site visit

What comprises a site visit?

In face-to-face and telephonic meetings, the grantmakers will want to hear from your team members in their own words about the project. They may ask in advance that each person summarize a component of the proposal or some variation thereof. Be especially prepared to answer questions on sustainability and evaluation.

In a face-to-face visit, the grantmakers may want to visit the agency where the project will take place. In that event, you should prepare the individuals who will be present during the visit so they can answer questions. Since these individuals may be somewhat remote from the proposal's intent, you cannot expect them to be experts, but they should be prepared well enough to speak to how the project may help solve the problem.

Finally, in each type of visit, you can expect to get questions about your proposal. The readers may not understand certain parts, or there may be gaps in what you have written. You and your team are the experts on the proposed project, and you should be able to answer any questions they pose. In the event that they ask something you cannot answer, you are better off indicating that you do not know the answer. In other words, be honest with your answers. If there is an opportunity to provide clarification after the site visit, offer to get back with them on the subject.

> **TIP**
> Make certain that all team members are well acquainted with the visit agenda and their role.

How can you improve your chances for funding?

"The price of success is hard work, dedication to the job at hand, and the determination that whether we win or lose, we have applied the best of ourselves to the task at hand."

—Vince Lombardi

The site visit is the golden opportunity to highlight your project and convince the grantmakers that their money will be well spent on your project. Follow a few simple rules:

* Mind your manners. Adhere to time limits and other requirements as expressed by the grantmaker, such as travel, lodging, and how much interaction with project personnel will be permitted. Start and end on time. Be polite and never adversarial.

* Show solidarity and camaraderie among the project partners. This is your dog-and-pony show to demonstrate why the project is important and how you intend to execute it. Include all partners who are well versed in the project; prime them prior to the visit. For solidarity, I relate the following story:

> In the 1990s, I was involved in a national program that used reverse site visits for the semifinalists. We invited a proposal team that traveled by van several hundred miles to the visit. They showed up wearing sweatshirts with the name of their project emblazoned on the front. In addition to demonstrating their sense of humor, they all looked like they were having a good time. They also were interchangeably familiar with the project, answering questions at will. Their project was funded.

* Demonstrate intimate familiarity with the project. Appoint people who have the most expertise to address each component of the project.

Enjoy your site visit. Demonstrate that you will be the best stewards of the grantmaker's money.

What can you expect to happen after the site visit?

You have done your best. You know that your project is on the short list for funding. Now you wait for the final decision.

FAQs

 Should I be worried if I receive notice that our project will have a site visit?

No! The notice is good news; it means that your proposal has made it into the semifinalist round.

 In your opinion, what is the most important part of the site visit?

Evidence that the project partners are working together and mutually committed to the proposed project.

 In your opinion, what is the least important part of the site visit?

The refreshments, although they are helpful.

 Can the site visit be a game changer, in either direction (funding or not funding)?

Yes, a somewhat poorly constructed proposal might be pushed over into an affirmative decision if the pieces come together during a site visit. This means that the partners work well together, that they all understand what they plan to do and the impact it will have on the targeted population, and that they possess the competencies to make the project happen. Conversely, a well-written proposal may not be selected if the opposite is evident—the partners are not well informed or committed, and there is little evidence that they possess the skills they need to bring the project to life.

References

Gladwell, M. (2005). *Blink: The power of thinking without thinking.* New York: Little, Brown, and Company.

TAKE-AWAY TIPS

✓ Receiving notice of a site visit is a good thing. It means that your proposal has made it into the semifinal round.

✓ Be overprepared for your site visit. Anticipate questions and develop answers.

✓ Learn as much as possible beforehand about your visitors.

✓ During a site visit, do not hesitate to demonstrate camaraderie among your partners and your knowledge of the project.

✓ Site visits are kind of like accreditation visits (JCAHO, CCNE, NLN—you get the picture). People show up and ask questions. They may look at where you will be carrying out your project. You want to be on your best behavior.

✓ Like accreditation visits, if you have a really good visit with no apparent deficiencies, you will be one step closer to receiving funding.

10

✳

Awaiting the Decision and Planning Next Steps

Do you:

Know how to forge forward when you receive an award letter?

Know how to respond to a rejection letter?

Know how to build on your assets and convert weaknesses for your next submission?

In this chapter, we cover your initial steps when you learn of the decision to fund or not to fund your project. Either way, you have decisions to make regarding your next steps. Obviously, you hope to receive an award letter. With the award come responsibilities for moving the project forward. If you receive a rejection letter, you want to learn how to improve your proposal for the next submission. Rejection is not finality; it's merely an object lesson on the road to success.

Glossary

Award: Notice from a grantmaker about receipt of funds to support a project.

Rejection: Notice from a grantmaker that funds have not been awarded to a proposal.

The award letter

"A dream doesn't become reality through magic; it takes sweat, determination, and hard work."

–Colin Powell

What comprises the award letter?

Hooray for you! If the grantor selects your project for funding, you will receive notice by phone, e-mail, and/or letter. You will be thrilled—not only because others believe in your proposed work and are willing to fund it, but also because you worked hard for this, and the award is ample recognition of the achievement. In addition, you will also be somewhat anxious, because now you will be held accountable for your ideas and proposed solution. Consequently, any thoughts you had about the proposed work in the abstract are now transitioning to the concrete and to action. Let's examine your next steps, using the example in Chapter 4 on a project involving pain assessment.

First, look carefully at the award letter. Box 10.1 contains a sample award letter based on the example in Chapter 4, and I've italicized and called out several key words—impact, budget, project goal, project partners, and program officer—to serve as a review of how critically important the written proposal is in the process of earning a grant award. Box 10.2 explores the key words in more detail.

Dear Awardee:

Congratulations! The XYZ Foundation has awarded your proposal, Pain Management Improvement, a grant of $25,000! You will receive your award in two equal payments 6 months apart, with the first check for $12,500 to be mailed June 1.

A *Impact* and *project goal* imply that the funding organization determined there was congruence between the intent of the project (the goal) and the impact on the targeted population.

We applaud you for tackling this clinical problem, and we agree that a research-based approach to developing and testing an assessment tool should have a lasting *impact* on patient comfort and quality of care. **A**

In a separate letter, we will communicate the requirements for receiving the award from our foundation. In addition, we had several **B** questions about your *budget* request, and we would like to speak with you in the near future by conference call to answer our questions and assure that you will be allocating our funds appropriately to meet your *project goal.* **A**

B Expect the award letter to reference the grant amount and the *budget* accountability associated with the award.

Since the XYZ Foundation will be announcing these awards publicly in the near future, we ask you to limit your communications to your **C** project partners. Once we have completed notifying all grantees in this grant cycle, we will issue a regional press release and create a template for you to use in your agency's public relations efforts.

C Identifying *project partners* highlights the importance of including stakeholders in the project, not only as idea generators in developing the proposal's work but also in terms of their willingness to contribute resources to the project.

We look forward to working with you. Your *program officer* is **D** Jane Smith, and her e-mail address is jane.smith@xyzfoundation.org. Do not hesitate to contact her with any questions you have concerning reporting requirements and other grant specifics.

D The *program officer* will be the point person at the foundation.

Thank you for your work on this proposal and commitment to the complex issues concerning pain assessment and management. We look forward to working with you.

(10.2) Key grant award terms

* *Impact* and *project goal* imply that the foundation looked critically at the logic model and determined that there was congruence between what the intent of the project is (the goal) and what the proposal writer determined to be the ultimate impact on the targeted population.

* Identifying *project partners* highlights the importance of including stakeholders in the project, not only as idea generators in developing the proposal's work but also in terms of their willingness to contribute resources to the project. As I've highlighted throughout this book, writing proposals is a team sport, and this award letter reinforces how important partners are to the effort.

* The award letter is, after all, about an "award" of money to support the project. Hence, *budget* is the reflection of the importance of money. When developing a proposal, the team identifies the activities to bring life to the project's goals. Each activity carries a cost, and this is reflected in the budget, including how much project partners will invest and the request from the grantor. Consequently, you can expect that the award letter will reference the grant amount and the accountability associated with the award. In the example in Box 10.1, XYZ Foundation notes that it has questions for the awardee about the budget. These questions are not deal breakers; the foundation has already indicated that it will award the grant. The questions mean that the awardee may need to rework the budget to meet the grantor's expectations. This is not a problem.

* Finally, the letter contains reference to the *program officer*, who will be the point person at the foundation. In Chapter 3, we discussed the importance of creating relationships with grantmakers. The awardee may already know the program officer, if the applicant sought and received technical assistance during the process of writing the proposal. If that is the case, consider the preparatory work properly executed. If not, start working on developing a relationship with the program officer from the day you receive the award notice.

TIP

Look closely at the award letter. It highlights the grantmaker's requirements to assure that the award will be well spent.

What work should we begin immediately?

"No business can succeed in any great degree without being properly organized."

—James Cash Penney

The first month or so of your project lays the foundation for your project's success. You will want to create an organizational structure that will execute the project's objectives. Box 10.3 guides you in getting started.

TIP Your award letter serves as the starting point for work on your project. Focus on organizing and establishing communication with partners and the grantmaker.

10.3

✳ **Notify your partners.** You want them to hear about the success of their collaborative efforts directly from you. Send them a copy of the award letter. Outline your thoughts about next steps, to include setting up a time for the partners to meet and organize the work at hand.

✳ **Consult your proposal for the timeline of activities to be performed on receipt of award.** These activities will most likely be associated with setting up the infrastructure that will coordinate project activities and might include hiring project personnel, setting up an office and acquiring office supplies and hardware, and establishing a means for communication among project personnel and partners.

✳ **Meet with the program officer and/or grantmaker's fiscal administrator.** This meeting can take place through conference call, and it will establish procedures for working with the grantmaker. Remember: The foundation wants you to succeed—success means that you should make a lasting impact on your targeted population. It also means that the grantmaker has chosen wisely and gives it bragging rights for investing in your project. Working collaboratively with the foundation is extremely important.

You are now well on your way toward a successful project. Congratulations and best wishes!

The rejection letter

"Don't let anyone, or any rejection, keep you from what you want."

–Ashley Tisdale

Treat the rejection letter as the beginning of a learning process for proposal improvement. Some grantmakers will identify broadly the areas that were found to be insufficient to receive funding. Others will offer little feedback. Your task will be to gather as much information about the reasons for rejection as you can, and develop a plan for improving your proposal for resubmission.

What are the reasons that projects are not funded?

Sometimes projects are not funded because there are insufficient funds to support all the worthy proposals that have been submitted. In other words, you may have written an excellent proposal that might have been funded under other funding cycles. In addition, there is always a human factor over which you have no control, and you will not realize that the human factor intervened in your project not being funded. For example, your proposal might be read by a reviewer whose expertise lies precisely in your strategies for solving the problem identified in your proposal. And, this person might not agree with your proposed solution, despite its merits. Instead of recusing himself from the deliberations for conflict of interest, the reviewer might assign a lower score to your proposal than to others. Other reviewers might

TIP Treat a rejection letter as an object lesson. Do not take it personally, although that is sometimes difficult to do. For one reason or another, your proposal failed to make the cut. But you can improve it for the future.

defer to this person's expertise as well. This is unfortunate, but the human element is always present, and sometimes it fails to work in your favor.

These situations aside, the vast majority of proposals are not funded for one or more of the reasons listed below.

* Failure to adhere to the structural requirements (page length, margins, font). Shame on you if this happens. You must pay attention to the grantmaker's rules.

* Incongruence with the grantmaker's funding requests. You have submitted a proposal that is inconsistent with the grant-maker's mission or funding priorities. This mistake should not happen, but it happens more often than one would think. Individuals become so convinced that their proposed work is worthy of funding, regardless of what the funders indicate they will fund. Instead of seeking another funder, the proposal writer attempts to fit that square screw into the round hole. It never works.

* Failure to demonstrate a need for the project. Your project may be worthy, and there may indeed be a need for it. But you have failed to demonstrate it. This happens in at least three ways: (1) You have supporting information, but you failed to write it in your proposal (or substantiate it in the site visit, if you participated in one); (2) you failed to provide sufficient data to support the need, either through lack of a survey or reported clinical measures; or (3) your literature review was flawed and failed to support a need for the problem.

* Lack of support from stakeholders. As I have identified throughout this book, project partners are critical to support the proposed project. Your proposal must indicate robust sup-port from partners, through letters and match or in-kind sup-port of the budget.

* Weakness in developing one or more sections of the proposal, such as the project narrative, work plan, deliverables, evalua-tion plan, or methods to sustain the project post-funding. The most common errors of incomplete proposal development are

the sustainability and evaluation plans. Proposal writers often have difficulty in projecting how they will sustain their work post-funding. Refer to Chapter 5. The evaluation plan can also prove vexing at times, if you do not possess strengths in evaluation. Refer to Chapter 6.

* Failure to demonstrate ability to carry out the project. This weakness is demonstrated through lack of qualified project personnel, insufficient support from administrators or project partners, and/or a budget that is unrealistic to meet the project objectives. Your description of the project personnel should be sufficient to demonstrate their expertise. If you will be hiring personnel, you should have submitted a job description that contained the requisite competencies. Administrators and project partners demonstrate their commitment through their letters of support, and you may not have obtained strong, individualized letters. Finally, your budget must be realistic, and if you have not sought or obtained sufficient funding to support your project, you may not be approved for funding.

* Internal inconsistencies in the proposal. Because proposals contain many components, opportunities abound for inconsistencies to emerge. This is especially true when various team members write different sections of the proposal. While I believe that team writing is important for success in proposal development, someone has to take responsibility for making certain that the proposal components are internally consistent with one another. You do not want to submit a proposal that has an objective and action steps for which there are no budgeted expenses. Alternatively, you do not want to list a person as a coordinator of activities with no responsibilities attached to that person in your action steps or work plan. Those are precisely the types of inconsistencies that will lower your score and possibly lead to a rejection letter.

TIP

Critically review your proposal, seeking answers for a rejection.

What should you do when you receive a rejection letter?

"If you're not making mistakes, you're not taking risks, and that means you re not going anywhere. The key is to make mistakes faster than the competition, so you have more chances to learn and win."

—John W. Holt, Jr.

After licking your wounds, take the following steps. These are designed to clarify your level of perseverance, determine if your partners remain committed to the project, and find out as much as you can about the reasons for your rejection.

First, take some time to evaluate your own and your partners' commitment to the project. It seemed like a good idea at the time, but is it still as important for you as it was when you started down this path? If the answer continues to be in the affirmative, and if you can picture yourself still as excited about the project after you rewrite the proposal, then talk with your partners. You will still need partners to carry out your work, although all may not want to continue. You will need to assess their commitment—in time and in match or in-kind support. If you lose partners, will you be able to find others to take their place?

Second, you will want to find out as much as you can about why your proposal was not funded. If you have developed relationships with individuals who work for the grantmaker, contact them and ask for the reasons. Indicate that you want to learn and want to improve the proposal so it can be considered in the future. The best case scenario will be that the

TIP

Remember, you are on a journey toward project improvement; the more information you can glean from multiple sources, the better.

grantmaker will share your proposal weaknesses with you and suggest ways to improve your chances in the future. Learn from your mistakes.

Third, find out who was funded (your grantmaker contact should be able to tell you this), and contact the individuals who received awards. You can ask to read their proposals, which they may or may not share, but at least find out as much as you can from them.

FAQs

 If I receive an award letter, may I request that changes be made in any components of the project before starting to work on it?

Yes, so long as you are not proposing to change the intent of the project, you may request changes. Things happen, even from the time of submission until you learn that your project will be funded. Explain the need for change with your program officer.

 Do grantmakers ever award more or less money than you have asked for?

Yes to both situations. Situations change for grantmakers, and they may have more or less money available to fund your project. The preferable scenario would be to have more money, but if you are offered less, figure out what changes you will need to make, and negotiate these with the grantmaker.

 If I receive a rejection letter, should I abandon all hope of obtaining funds for my project?

Of course not. Most grantwriters are very lucky if they get funded on their first attempt. Proposals have many parts, and a weakness in any one part might be the difference between your proposal being funded and another person's being funded. Your job is to find out why you were not funded and improve on the product.

TAKE-AWAY TIPS

✓ Being awarded funds for resolving a problem is affirmation that you convinced the funder that your project is worthy. Now you are responsible for putting your words into action.

✓ Communicate early and often with your project partners and the contacts within your funding agency. You will increase the likelihood of success by actively involving them in the project.

✓ Organize your project. This includes holding meetings with established agendas, adhering to timelines or adjusting them with good cause, and keeping your eye on the goal and objectives. No one likes to work on disorganized projects. Don't let it happen.

✓ Treat a rejection as an opportunity for growth. Find out what went wrong, assess your will to persevere, and get back to work.

Glossary

Activities, a.k.a. action steps: Each of the project steps planned in conducting the project. Each step is one part of a series of steps toward achieving a certain outcome. Some activities will also produce outputs (W. K. Kellogg Foundation, 2006).

Applicant: An organization seeking grant funds for a specific project.

Assumptions: Beliefs we have about the project, the people involved, and the context and the way we think the project will work (W. K. Kellogg Foundation, 2006). Assumptions form the foundation or are the preconditions existing before beginning a change project.

Biographical information: Information on project personnel named in the budget. Funders may provide a form to use for this information.

Budget narrative: Description of how funds will be expended to meet project objectives. The narrative should complement and be consistent with the proposal narrative.

Budget: How the applicant will spend the award. This usually consists of a table outlining the expense components such as project staff, supplies, equipment, travel and meetings, and consultants/contracted personnel. In addition, this section may also require a budget narrative that explains how each of the expenses will contribute to the project goals and outcomes.

Call or request for proposals (commonly abbreviated as CFP or RFP): A document that describes a project and seeks applicants to submit a written response detailing their plan to carry out the specifics of the project.

Collaboration: A process by which individuals with differing perspectives on a problem agree to work together on solutions.

Computer hardware and office equipment: Some funders require that these outlays are itemized and explained fully so that their purchase can be deemed essential to the operation of the project. When it comes to purchasing technology tools, some funders may require a description of the time the computer will be used specifically for the project. Funders can require that the budget amount requested represent the percentage of time for which the technology will be used for the project.

Consultant/contract expenses: These expenses are usually calculated at a flat or hourly rate and are contracted out of the agency without any fringe benefits.

Concept paper: A brief overview of a subject.

Context evaluation: Collection of data to determine the worth of a project or the need for the project.

Direct costs: Costs that can be assigned to a specific cost center. In grantmaking, direct costs usually refer to personnel and fringe benefits.

Eligibility criteria: Tax status of applicant agency requirements. Usually government or public entities and nonprofit organizations that are tax-exempt under Section 501(c)(3) of the Internal Revenue Code. The funder may place other requirements as well, such as location of the applicant, population demographics, poverty, rurality, type of educational program.

Evaluation: Systematic method for collecting, analyzing, and using information to answer questions about a project.

External factors: Environment in which the project exists, includes a variety of external factors that interact with and influence project action. External factors are more likely than not variables over which you have no or little control.

Giving circle: A form of philanthropy consisting of groups of individuals who pool their funds and resources to donate to their communities (www.michiganfoundations.org/s_cmf/sec.asp).

Goal, a.k.a. objective, or long-term objective, or impact: The intended aim or impact over the life of the project. For each action in a project, you should answer the question "How will this affect the goal we are trying to achieve?"

Grantmaker: An organization that makes a grant. Also called grantor.

Grant: A sum of money given to an organization for a specific purpose.

Grantee: The recipient of a grant.

Impact: The desired endpoint of the project. See "goal."

In-kind (or contributed) costs: These are contributions from your agency and other partners. Some funders require a certain "match" such as a 1:1 match, meaning that you seek $1 in funding for every $1 that is donated to the project. In-kind costs are typically "donated" from agencies, such as paying for a person's time allocated to the project or other donations such as meeting space, refreshments, and so forth. Other costs are contributed, such as real cash.

Income: Funds that accrue to the agency as a result of project activity, such as tuition charges.

Indirect costs: A portion of the funder's grant allocation that is used to operate the project for such items as office space and overhead. Some funders do not permit any grant funds to be used for indirect costs. Others cap the costs at a certain percent or amount.

Input evaluation: Assessment of the components of a project that are integral to the foundation of the project, such as the assumptions and external environment. Used interchangeably with context evaluation.

Inputs, a.k.a. resources: Resources, contributions, and investments that comprise the means by which a project is achieved.

Key words: Words or phrases the use of which in a call for proposals takes on a level of priority. These words or phrases may appear in **bold** or *italics* or may be used frequently in the funders' materials or proposal.

Letters of support: Documentation of agreement and participation from stakeholders, such as proposed project staff and partners, memoranda of understanding, letters from community leaders affirming need and capacity of your organization to manage a grant.

Line-item budget: The project budget laid out in spreadsheet format. The funder may require use of specific forms or subsections. Include both requested funds and funds that will be in-kind or match to meet the funder's requirements.

Literature ("lit") review: a process of reading, analyzing, evaluating, and summarizing scholarly materials about a specific topic.

Logic model: Systematic and visual way to present and share one's understanding of the relationships among resources used to operate a project, activities planned, and changes or intended results. Displays the sequence of actions that describe what a project is and will do: how investments link to results. The logic model has five core components: inputs, outputs, outcomes, assumptions, and external factors (W. K. Kellogg Foundation, 2006).

Needs assessment: A process for gathering information about current conditions within a population that underlie the need for an intervention (www.epa.gov/evaluate/glossary/all-esd.htm). Usually forms the basis for an intervention plan.

Needs assessment: A systematic process to acquire information on a subject that includes the strengths and weaknesses.

Nonpersonnel direct costs: The amount of grant funding allocated toward the direct operation of the funded project, such as meeting and travel expenses, printing and copying, and computer software.

Nonprofit tax status: Not subject to taxation. In grantmaking, includes organizations exempt from taxes under the IRS code 501(c)(3); public schools, colleges, and universities; and other state and local governmental agencies.

Outcomes, a.k.a. objectives: In some models, objectives are identified as short-term, intermediate, and long-term outcomes. Results or changes for individuals, groups, communities, organizations, or systems (W. K. Kellogg Foundation, 2006). The changes expected to result from a project—changes among clients, communities, systems, or organizations.

Outputs, a.k.a. deliverables: Activities, services, events, and products that reach people who participate in the project or who are targeted. These are usually quantifiable. For example, how many participants attended a workshop, what materials were developed in the course of the project, were minutes kept of project meetings?

Personnel: The amount of funding allocated toward compensating project personnel who are part of the funded agency. Personnel costs are generally calculated based on the person's time devoted to the project as a percent of that person's salary, plus a prorated portion of his or her fringe benefits.

Philanthropy: The desire to promote the welfare of others, usually expressed by a donation of money to good causes.

Problem statement, a.k.a. issue statement or situation: A description of the problem that the project seeks to solve.

Process evaluation: Assessment of activities designed to achieve project objectives.

Product evaluation: Assessment of data collected to determine the effectiveness of the project in meeting its outcomes or achieving intended impact.

Proposal narrative: The main body of the proposal that describes each required section of the proposal.

Proposal: A term used to describe an intention or a plan to accomplish something.

Purpose: The intent of the project. Examples: research to solve a clinical problem, an innovation project such as testing a new strategy for smoking cessation, replication or expansion of a successful program using a different population or location, or development/implementation of educational content to meet a growing need.

Selection criteria: The items that must be included in the proposal.

Series of "if-then" relationships: The relationships that connect the components of the logic model: *if* resources are available to the project, *then* project activities can be implemented; *if* project activities are implemented successfully, *then* certain outputs and outcomes can be expected; *if* the project achieves the desired outcomes, *then* it will accomplish the intended impact on the targeted population.

SMART: Acronym used as qualifiers for writing outcomes (objectives) and impacts (goals): Specific * Measurable * Action-oriented * Realistic * Timed (ChangingMinds.org, nd).

Submission requirements: A description of the details for submission, such as length of the proposal, margins, font, spacing, and what can be included in an appendix.

Summative evaluation: See product evaluation.

Support letters: Communication from each project partner, outlining the role played in proposal development and the role to be played, should funding be awarded.

Technical assistance: Help and advice provided on a specialized subject matter (www.nonprofitsassistancefund.org/index.php).

Transmittal letter: Introductory letter from either the project director or the chief administrative officer of the agency.

Useful Grantwriting Internet Links

www.ahrq.gov/fund/ — The Agency for Healthcare Research and Quality funds projects focused on comparative effectiveness research, prevention and care management, value in health care (reducing inefficiencies and redundancies), health information technology, patient safety, and emerging/innovative issues.

www.doleta.gov — The Employment and Training Administration of the U.S. Department of Labor is the agency that administers grants for job training and worker dislocation projects. Occasionally, grants are available to improve worker performance, such as conflict resolution in the work environment.

http://essayplant.com/conceptpaperwriting.php — This site contains a nice primer on concept paper writing. Simple to understand.

http://evi.sagepub.com/content/11/4/447.short — Abstract to an article on evaluation designs and models that can be adapted for different types of projects. The full article costs $25.

www.federalgrantswire.com — This site is a free resource for federal grants, but it is not a government-run site. You can search by federal agency, subject area, or use the Google search box where you can put in your key words to search for funding sources. Once you click on a subject, the site will take you to a description of the project, its status, grant objectives (read this carefully for key words), use of funds and funding restrictions, eligibility requirements, application procedures, and deadlines, with a hyperlink to the federal agency in charge of the grant project.

www.grants.gov/search/category.do — Grants.gov is the website that lists all federal grant opportunities. On this selected page, you can search by category (education, environment, health) and obtain a listing of all open grant opportunities.

www.grants.gov/applicants/email_subscription.jsp — This page contains information on how to register for grants RSS feeds and grant updates and notices.

www.hrsa.gov — The Health Resources and Services Administration (HRSA) of the U.S. Department of Health and Human Services is the primary federal agency for access to health care services for people who are uninsured, isolated, or medically vulnerable. HRSA is composed of six bureaus and nine offices, all of which are described on the HRSA website.

http://marthabianco.com/Courses/Cities/concept.html — Academic in nature. Begins with the research process (including a rather convoluted schema on the process of research). The information on writing a concept paper is found under number 5. Useful if you want more information on how the concept paper integrates into the research process, apart from grantwriting.

www.rwjf.org — The Robert Wood Johnson Foundation is the nation's largest philanthropy devoted solely to the public's health. The Foundation has a rich history of funding nursing-related projects.

www.tophealthgrants.com — A listing of recent and active grants.

www.uml.edu/centers/cfwc/Community_Tips/Grant_Writing/Concept_Paper. html — A one-pager on how to write a one-pager. The author, Beata Murrell, also includes a link on how to succeed at grantwriting by doing thorough background research.

www.uml.edu/centers/cfwc/Community_Tips/Grant_Writing/ networking.html — This is a brief piece on networking to find funds. It contains a wonderful list of things to do when looking for and engaging partners in your venture.

www.wkkf.org — The W. K. Kellogg Foundation funds health-related projects nationally and internationally focused on health, agriculture, and education.

www.wmich.edu/evalctr/checklists/evaluation-models/ — Evaluation model checklists from the Evaluation Center at Western Michigan University. This site has links to the CIPP model and other evaluation types.

Index

SMART acronym, 48, 140
state government grants, 31–32
submission of proposal. See also call for proposals (CFP)
    budget narrative, 90, 99, 102, 135
    by mail, 105
    electronic, 105
    in person, 106
    line-item budget, 90–91, 99, 102, 138
    meeting deadline, 105, 111–112
    project narrative, 99, 102
    requirements, 140
        grantmaker forms, 103
        number of copies, 103
        structural, 103, 111
        transmittal letter, 102, 104, 140
    reviewing, 109–111
    supporting materials
        appendices, 108–109
        biographical information, 107
        eligibility, 40–41, 64, 66–67, 106–107, 136
        letters of support, 64, 102, 108, 111–113, 138, 140
        partner identification, 107
        personnel identification, 107
    tips, 111
summative evaluation, 81–82, 85, 140
surveys, 17–18, 52

target, 5
tax-exempt status, 27, 30, 40–41, 64, 66, 106, 136, 138
team
    leadership, 62
    recruiting, 49, 60–61
    roles, 50, 60
    skills needed, 48–49
    whom to invite, 48–49
teamwork. See collaboration
technical assistance
    definition, 2, 140
    to applicants, 7, 10
    website, 2
transmittal letter, 102, 104, 140

U.S. Department of Health and Human Services, 32, 34, 142

W. K. Kellogg Foundation websites, 35, 143
websites
    Agency for Healthcare Research and Quality, 141
    Community Foundations, 30
    concept papers, 20, 141
    Employment and Training Administration, 141
    evaluation designs and models, 141
    evaluation model checklists, 143
    federal funding resources, 33–34, 141–142
    finding grantmakers, 30
    giving circle, 2
    Health Resources and Services Administration (HRSA), 142
    list of recent grants, 142
    national funding resources, 35
    needs assessment, 2
    networking, 142
    research process, 142
    Robert Wood Johnson Foundation, 142
    RSS feeds, updates for grants, 142
    technical assistance, 2
    W. K. Kellogg Foundation, 35, 143
    writing one-pager, 142
working with others. See collaboration